COCOA AND CHOCOLATE

Arthur W. Knapp

Cocoa and Chocolate, by Arthur W. Knapp

Title: Cocoa and Chocolate Their History from Plantation to Consumer

Author: Arthur W. Knapp

Release Date: August 18, 2006 [EBook #19073]

Language: English

Character set encoding: ISO-8859-1

COCOA AND CHOCOLATE

Their History from Plantation to Consumer

By

ARTHUR W. KNAPP B. Sc. (B'ham.), F.I.C., B. Sc. (Lond.)
Member of the Society of Public Analysts; Member of the Society of Chemical Industry; Fellow of the Institute of Hygiene.
Research Chemist to Messrs. Cadbury Bros., Ltd.

LONDON CHAPMAN AND HALL, LTD. 1920

PREFACE

Although there are several excellent scientific works dealing in a detailed manner with the cacao bean and its products from the various view points of the technician, there is no comprehensive modern work written for the general reader. Until that appears, I offer this little book, which attempts to cover lightly but accurately the whole ground, including the history of cacao, its cultivation and manufacture. This is a small book in which to treat of so large a subject, and to avoid prolixity I have had to generalise. This is a dangerous practice, for what is gained in brevity is too often lost in accuracy: brevity may be always the soul of wit, it is rarely the body of truth. The expert will find that I have considered him in that I have given attention to recent developments, and if I have talked of the methods peculiar to one place as though they applied to the whole world, I ask him to consider me by supplying the inevitable variations and exceptions himself.

The book, though short, has taken me a long time to write, having been written in the brief breathing spaces of a busy life, and it would never have been completed but for the encouragement I received from Messrs. Cadbury Bros., Ltd., who aided me in every possible way. I am particularly indebted to the present Lord Mayor of Birmingham, Mr. W.A. Cadbury, for advice and criticism, and to Mr. Walter Barrow for reading the proofs. The members of the staff to whom I am indebted are Mr. W. Pickard, Mr. E.J. Organ, Mr. T.B. Rogers; also Mr. A. Hackett, for whom the diagrams in the manufacturing section were originally made by Mr. J.W. Richards. I am grateful to Messrs. J.S. Fry and Sons, Limited, for information and photographs. In one or two cases I do not know whom to thank for the photographs, which have been culled from many sources. I have much pleasure in thanking the following: Mr. R. Whymper for a large number of Trinidad photos; the Director of the Imperial Institute and Mr. John Murray for permission to use three illustrations from the Imperial Institute series of handbooks to the Commercial Resources of the Tropics; M. Ed. Leplae, Director-General of Agriculture, Belgium, for several photos, the blocks of which were kindly supplied by Mr. H. Hamel Smith, of Tropical Life; Messrs. Macmillan and Co. for five reproductions from C.J.J. van Hall's book on Cocoa; and West Africa for four illustrations of the Gold Coast.

The photographs reproduced on pages 2, 23, 39, 47, 49 and 71 are by Jacobson of Trinidad, on pages 85 and 86 by Underwood & Underwood of London, and on page 41 by Mrs. Stanhope Lovell of Trinidad.

The industry with which this book deals is changing slowly from an art to a science. It is in a transition period (it is one of the humours of any live industry that it is always in a transition period). There are many indications of scientific progress in cacao cultivation; and now that, in addition to the experimental and research departments attached to the principal firms, a Research Association has been formed for the cocoa and chocolate industry, the increased amount of diffused scientific knowledge of cocoa and chocolate manufacture should give rise to interesting developments.

A.W. KNAPP.

Birmingham, *February, 1920.*

CONTENTS

CHAPTER I

COCOA AND CHOCOLATE--A SKETCH OF THEIR HISTORY 5

CHAPTER II

CACAO AND ITS CULTIVATION 17

CHAPTER III

HARVESTING AND PREPARATION FOR THE MARKET 45
With a dialogue on "The Kind of Cacao the Manufacturers Like."

CHAPTER IV

CACAO PRODUCTION AND SALE 81 With notes on the chief producing areas, cacao markets, and the planter's life

CHAPTER V

THE MANUFACTURE OF COCOA AND CHOCOLATE 119

CHAPTER VI

THE MANUFACTURE OF CHOCOLATE 139

CHAPTER VII

BY-PRODUCTS OF THE COCOA AND CHOCOLATE INDUSTRY 157 (*a*) Cacao Butter, (*b*) Cacao Shell

CHAPTER VIII

THE COMPOSITION AND FOOD VALUE OF COCOA AND CHOCOLATE 165 (including Milk Chocolate)

CHAPTER IX

ADULTERATION, AND THE NEED FOR DEFINITIONS 179

CHAPTER X

LIST OF ILLUSTRATIONS

marked Raking Cacao Beans on the Driers, Ecuador Gathering Cacao Pods, Ecuador Sorting Cacao for Shipment, Ecuador MAP of South America and the West Indies Workers on a Cacao Plantation MAP of Africa, with only Cacao-Producing Areas marked Foreshore at Accra, with Stacks of Cacao ready for Shipment Carriers conveying Bags of Cacao to Surf Boats, Accra Crossing the River, Gold Coast Drying Cacao Beans, Gold Coast Shooting Cacao from the Road to the Beach, Accra Rolling Cacao, Gold Coast Rolling Cacao, Gold Coast Carrying Cacao to the Railway Station, Gold Coast Wagon Loads of Cacao being taken from Depot to the Beach, Accra The Buildings of the Boa Entrada Cacao Estate, San Thomé Drying Cacao, San Thomé Barrel Rolling, Gold Coast Bagging Cacao, Gold Coast Surf Boats by the Side of the Ocean Liner, Accra Bagging Cacao Beans for Shipment, Trinidad Transferring Bags of Cacao to Lighters, Trinidad Diagram showing Variation in Price of Cacao Beans, 1913-1919 Group of Workers on Cacao Estate Carting Cacao to Railway Station, Ceylon The Carenage, Grenada Early Factory Methods Women Grinding Chocolate Cacao Bean Warehouse Cacao Bean Sorting and Cleaning Machine Diagram of Cacao Bean Cleaning Machine Section through Gas Heated Cacao Roaster Roasting Cacao Beans Cacao Bean, Shell and Germ Section through Kibbling Cones and Germ Screens Section through Winnowing Machine Cacao Grinding Section through Grinding Stones A Cacao Press Section through Cacao Press-pot and Ram-plate Chocolate Mélangeur Plan of Chocolate Mélangeur Chocolate Refining Machine Grinding Cacao Nib and Sugar Section through Chocolate Grinding Rolls "Conche" Machines Section through "Conche" Machine Machines for Mixing or "Conching" Chocolate Chocolate Shaking Table Girls Covering or Dipping Cremes, etc. The Enrober A Confectionery Room Factory at which Milk is Evaporated for Milk Chocolate Manufacture Cocoa and Chocolate Despatch Deck Boxing Chocolates Packing Chocolates Factory at which Milk is Evaporated for Milk Chocolate Manufacture Cacao Pods, Leaves and Flowers

INTRODUCTION

In a few short chapters I propose to give a plain account of the production of cocoa and chocolate. I assume that the reader is not a specialist and knows little or nothing of the subject, and hence both the style of writing and the treatment of the subject will be simple. At the same time, I assume that the reader desires a full and accurate account, and not a vague story in which the difficulties are ignored. I hope that, as a result of this method of dealing with my subject, even experts will find much in the book that is of interest and value. After a brief survey of the history of cocoa and chocolate, I shall begin with the growing of the cacao bean, and follow the *cacao* in its career until it becomes the finished product ready for consumption.

Cacao or Cocoa?

The reader will have noted above the spelling "cacao," and to those who think it curious, I would say that I do not use this spelling from pedantry. It is an imitation of the word which the Mexicans used for this commodity as early as 1500, and when spoken by Europeans is apt to sound like the howl of a dog. The Mexicans called the tree from which cacao is obtained *cacauatl*. When the great Swedish scientist Linnaeus, the father of botany, was naming and classifying (about 1735) the trees and plants known in his time, he christened it *Theobroma Cacao*, by which name it is called by botanists to this day. Theo-broma is Greek for "Food of the Gods." Why Linnaeus paid this extraordinary compliment to cacao is obscure, but it has been suggested that he was inordinately fond of the beverage prepared from it--the cup which both cheers and satisfies. It will be seen from the above that the species-name is cacao, and one can understand that Englishmen, finding it difficult to get their insular lips round this outlandish word, lazily called it cocoa.

[Illustration: CACAO PODS (Amelonado type) in various states of growth and ripeness.]

In this book I shall use the words cacao, cocoa, and chocolate as follows:

Cacao, when I refer to the cacao tree, the cacao pod, or the cacao bean or seed. By the single word, cacao, I imply the raw product, cacao beans, in bulk.

Cocoa, when I refer to the powder manufactured from the roasted bean by pressing out part of the butter. The word is too well established to be changed, even if one wished it. As we shall see later (in the chapter on adulteration) it has come legally to have a very definite significance. If this method of distinguishing between cacao and cocoa were the accepted practice, the perturbation which occurred in the public mind during the war (in 1916), as to whether manufacturers were exporting "cocoa" to neutral countries, would not have arisen. It should have been spelled "cacao," for the statements referred to the raw beans and not to the manufactured beverage. Had this been done, it would have been unnecessary for the manufacturers to point out that cocoa powder was not being so exported, and that they naturally did not sell the raw cacao bean.

Chocolate.--This word is given a somewhat wider meaning. It signifies any preparation of roasted cacao beans without abstraction of butter. It practically always contains sugar and added cacao butter, and is generally prepared in moulded form. It is used either for eating or drinking.

Cacao Beans and Coconuts.

In old manuscripts the word cacao is spelled in all manner of ways, but *cocoa* survived them all. This curious inversion, *cocoa*, is to be regretted, for it has led to a confusion which could not otherwise have arisen. But for this spelling no one would have dreamed of confusing the totally unrelated bodies, cacao and the milky coconut. (You note that I spell it "coconut," not "cocoanut," for the name is derived from the Spanish "coco," "grinning face," or bugbear for frightening children, and was given to the nut because the three scars at the broad end of the nut resemble a grotesque face). To make confusion worse confounded the old writers referred to cacao *seeds* as cocoa *nuts* (as for example, in *The Humble Memorial of Joseph Fry*, quoted in the chapter on history), but, as in appearance cacao seeds resemble *beans*, they are now usually spoken of as beans. The distinction between cacao and the coconut may be summarised thus:

Cacao. Coconut.

Botanical Name Theobroma Cacao Cocos nucifera Palm Tree Palm

Fruit Cacao pod, containing Coconut, which with outer many seeds (cacao beans) fibre is as large as a man's head

Products Cocoa Broken coconut (copra) Chocolate Coconut matting

Fatty Constituent Cacao butter Coconut oil

CHAPTER I

COCOA AND CHOCOLATE--A SKETCH OF THEIR HISTORY

Did time and space allow, there is much to be told on the romantic side of chocolate, of its divine origin, of the bloody wars and brave exploits of the Spaniards who conquered Mexico and were the first to introduce cacao into Europe, tales almost too thrilling to be believed, of the intrigues of the Spanish Court, and of celebrities who met and sipped their chocolate in the parlours of the coffee and chocolate houses so fashionable in the seventeenth and eighteenth centuries.

Cocoa and Chocolate (Whymper).

On opening a cacao pod, it is seen to be full of beans surrounded by a fruity pulp, and whilst the pulp is very pleasant to taste, the beans themselves are uninviting, so that doubtless the beans were always thrown away until ... someone tried roasting them. One pictures this "someone," a pre-historic Aztec with swart skin, sniffing the aromatic fume coming from the roasting beans, and thinking that beans which smelled so appetising must be good to consume. The name of the man who discovered the use of cacao must be written in some early chapter of the history of man, but it is blurred and unreadable: all we know is that he was an inhabitant of the New World and probably of Central America.

Original Home of Cacao.

The corner of the earth where the cacao tree originally grew, and still grows wild to-day, is the country watered by the mighty Amazon and the Orinoco. This is the very region in which Orellano, the Spanish adventurer, said that he had truly seen El Dorado, which he described as a City of Gold, roofed with gold, and standing by a lake with golden sands. In reality, El Dorado was nothing but a vision, a vision that for a hundred years fascinated all manner of dreamers and adventurers from Sir Walter Raleigh downwards, so that many braved great hardships in search of it, groped through the forests where the cacao tree grew, and returned to Europe feeling they had failed. To our eyes they were not entirely unsuccessful, for whilst they failed to find a city of gold, they discovered the home of the golden pod.

[Illustration: OLD DRAWING OF AN AMERICAN INDIAN; AT HIS FEET A CHOCOLATE-CUP, CHOCOLATE-POT, AND CHOCOLATE WHISK OR "MOLINET." (From *Traitez Nouveaux et Curieux du Café, du Thé, et du Chocolate*. Dufour, 1693).]

Montezuma--the First Great Patron of Chocolate.

When Columbus discovered the New World he brought back with him to Europe many new and curious things, one of which was cacao. Some years later, in 1519, the Spanish conquistador, Cortes, landed in Mexico, marched into the interior and discovered to his surprise, not the huts of savages, but a beautiful city, with palaces and museums. This city was the capital of the Aztecs, a remarkable people, notable alike for their ancient civilisation and their wealth. Their national drink was chocolate, and Montezuma, their Emperor, who lived in a state of luxurious magnificence, "took no other beverage than the chocolatl, a potation of chocolate, flavoured with vanilla and other spices, and so prepared as to be reduced to a froth of the consistency of honey, which gradually dissolved in the mouth and was taken cold. This beverage if so it could be called, was served in golden goblets, with spoons of the same metal or tortoise-shell finely wrought. The Emperor was exceedingly fond of it, to judge from the quantity--no less than fifty jars or pitchers being prepared for his own daily consumption: two thousand more were allowed for that of his household."[1] It is curious that Montezuma took no other beverage than chocolate, especially if it be true that the Aztecs also invented that fascinating drink, the cocktail (xoc-tl). How long this ancient people, students of the mysteries of culinary science, had known the art of preparing a drink from cacao, is not known, but it is evident that the cultivation of cacao received great attention in these parts, for if we read down the list of the tributes paid by different cities to the Lords of Mexico, we find "20 chests of ground chocolate, 20 bags of gold dust," again "80 loads of red chocolate, 20 lip-jewels of clear amber," and yet again "200 loads of chocolate."

[1] Prescott's *Conquest of Mexico*.

Another people that share with the Aztecs the honour of being the first great cultivators of cacao are the Incas of Peru, that wonderful nation that knew not poverty.

The Fascination of Chocolate.

That chocolate charmed the ladies of Mexico in the seventeenth century (even as it charms the ladies of England to-day) is shown by a story which Gage relates in his *New Survey of the West Indias* (1648). He tells us that at Chiapa, southward from Mexico, the women used to interrupt both sermon and mass by having their maids bring them a cup of hot chocolate; and when the Bishop, after fair warning, excommunicated them for this presumption, they changed their church. The Bishop, he adds, was poisoned for his pains.

Cacao Beans as Money.

Cacao was used by the Aztecs not only for the preparation of a beverage, but also as a circulating medium of exchange. For example, one could purchase a "tolerably good slave" for 100 beans. We read that: "Their currency consisted of transparent quills of gold dust, of bits of tin cut in the form of a T, and of bags of cacao containing a specified number of grains." "Blessed money," exclaims Peter Martyr, "which exempts its possessor from avarice, since it cannot be long hoarded, nor hidden underground!"

Derivation of Chocolate.

The word was derived from the Mexican *chocolatl*. The Mexicans used to froth their chocolatl with curious whisks made specially for the purpose (see page 6). Thomas Gage suggests that *choco, choco, choco* is a vocal representation of the sound made by stirring chocolate. The suffix *atl* means water. According to Mr. W.J. Gordon, we owe the name of chocolate to a misprint. He states that Joseph Acosta, who wrote as early as 1604 of chocolatl, was made by the printer to write *chocolaté*, from which the English eliminated the accent, and the French the final letter.

[Illustration: NATIVE AMERICAN INDIANS ROASTING AND GRINDING THE BEANS, AND MIXING THE CHOCOLATE IN A JUG WITH A WHISK. (From Ogilvy's *America*, 1671)]

First Cacao in Europe.

The Spanish discoverers of the New World brought home to Spain quantities of cacao, which the curious tasted. We may conclude that they drank the preparation cold, as Montezuma did, *hot* chocolate being a later invention. The new drink, eagerly sought by some, did not meet with universal approval, and, as was natural, the most diverse opinions existed as to the pleasantness and wholesomeness of the beverage when it was first known. Thus Joseph Acosta (1604) wrote: "The chief use of this cocoa is in a drincke which they call Chocholaté, whereof they make great account, foolishly and without reason; for it is loathsome to such as are not acquainted with it, having a skumme or frothe that is very unpleasant to taste, if they be not well conceited thereof. Yet it is a drincke very much esteemed among the Indians, whereof they feast noble men as they passe through their country. The Spaniards, both men and women, that are accustomed to the country are very greedy of this chocholaté." It is not impossible that the English, with the defeat of the Armada fresh in memory, were at first contemptuous of this "Spanish" drink. Certain it is, that when British sea-rovers like Drake and Frobisher, captured Spanish galleons on the high seas, and on searching their holds for treasure, found bags of cacao, they flung them overboard in scorn. In considering this scorn of cacao, shown alike by British buccaneers and Dutch corsairs, together with the critical air of Joseph Acosta, we should remember that the original chocolatl of the Mexicans consisted of a mixture of maize and cacao with hot spices like chillies, and contained no sugar. In this condition few inhabitants of the temperate zone could relish it. It however only needed one thing, the addition of sugar, and the introduction of this marked the beginning of its European popularity. The Spaniards were the first to manufacture and drink chocolate in any quantity. To this day they serve it in the old style--thick as porridge and pungent with spices. They endeavoured to keep secret the method of preparation, and, without success, to retain the manufacture as a monopoly. Chocolate was introduced into Italy by Carletti, who praised it and spread the method of its manufacture abroad. The new drink was introduced by monks from Spain into Germany and France, and when in 1660 Maria Theresa, Infanta of Spain, married Louis XIV, she made chocolate well known at the Court of France. She it was of whom a French historian wrote that Maria Theresa had only two passions--the king and chocolate.

Chocolate was advocated by the learned physicians of those times as a cure for many diseases, and it was stated that Cardinal Richelieu had been cured of general atrophy by its use.

From France the use of chocolate spread into England, where it began to be drunk as a luxury by the aristocracy about the time of the Commonwealth. It must have made some progress in public favour by 1673, for in that year "a Lover of his Country" wrote in the *Harleian Miscellany* demanding its prohibition (along with brandy, rum, and tea) on the ground that this imported article did no good and hindered the consumption of English-grown barley and wheat. New things appeal to the imaginative, and the absence of authentic knowledge concerning them allows free play to the imagination--so it happened that in the early days, whilst many writers vied with one another in writing glowing panegyrics on cacao, a few thought it an evil thing. Thus, whilst it was praised by many for its "wonderful faculty of quenching thirst, allaying hectic heats, of nourishing and fattening the body," it was seriously condemned by others as an inflamer of the passions!

Chocolate Houses and Clubs.

"The drinking here of chocolate Can make a fool a sophie."

In the spacious days of Queen Elizabeth, tea, coffee, and chocolate were unknown save to travellers and savants, and the handmaidens of the good queen drank beer with their breakfast. When Shakespeare and Ben Jonson forgathered at the Mermaid Tavern, their winged words passed over tankards of ale, but later other drinks became the usual accompaniment of news, story, and discussion. In the sixteen-sixties there were no strident newspapers to destroy one's equanimity, and the gossip of the day began to be circulated and discussed over cups of tea, coffee, or chocolate. The humorists, ever stirred by novelty, tilted, pen in hand, at these new drinks: thus one rhymster described coffee as

"Syrrop of soot or essence of old shoes."

The first coffee-house in London was started in St. Michael's Alley, Cornhill, in 1652 (when coffee was seven shillings a pound); the first tea-house was opened in Exchange Alley in 1657 (when tea was five sovereigns a pound), and in the same year (with chocolate about ten to fifteen shillings per pound) a Frenchman opened the first chocolate-house in Queen's Head Alley, Bishopsgate Street. The rising popularity of chocolate led to the starting of more of these chocolate houses, at which one could sit and sip chocolate, or purchase the commodity for preparation at home. Pepys' entry in his diary for 24th November, 1664, contains: "To a coffee house to drink jocolatte, very good." It is an artless entry, and yet one can almost hear him smacking his lips. Silbermann says that "After the Restoration there were shops in London for the sale of chocolate at ten shillings or fifteen shillings per pound. Ozinda's chocolate house was full of aristocratic consumers. Comedies, satirical essays, memoirs and private letters of that age frequently mention it. The habit of using chocolate was deemed a token of elegant and fashionable taste, and while the charms of this beverage in the reigns of Queen Anne and George I. were so highly esteemed by courtiers, by lords and ladies and fine gentlemen in the polite world, the learned physicians extolled its medicinal virtues." From the coffee house and its more aristocratic relative the chocolate house, there developed a new feature in English social life--the Club. As the years passed the Chocolate House remained a rendezvous, but the character of its habitués changed from time to time. Thus one, famous in the days of Queen Anne, and well known by its sign of the "Cocoa Tree," was at first the headquarters of the Jacobite party, and the resort of Tories of the strictest school. It became later a noted gambling house ("The gamesters shook their elbows in White's and the chocolate houses round Covent Garden," *National Review*, 1878), and ultimately developed into a literary club, including amongst its members Gibbon, the historian, and Byron, the poet.

Tax on Cacao.

The growing consumption of chocolate did not escape the all-seeing eye of the Chancellors of England. As early as 1660 we find amongst various custom and excise duties granted to Charles II:

"For every gallon of chocolate, sherbet, and tea made and sold, to be paid by the maker thereof ..... 8d."

Later the raw material was also made a source of revenue. In *The Humble Memorial of Joseph Fry*, of Bristol, Maker of Chocolate, which was addressed to the Lords Commissioners of the Treasury in 1776 (Messrs. Fry and Sons are the oldest English firm of chocolate makers, having been founded in 1728), we read that "Chocolate ... pays two shillings and threepence per pound excise, besides about ten shillings per hundredweight on the Cocoa Nuts from which it is made."

In 1784 a preferential customs rate was proposed in favour of our Colonies. This they enjoyed for many years before 1853, when the uniform rate, until recently in force, was introduced. This restrictive tariff on foreign growths rose in 1803 to 5s. 10d. per pound, against 1s. 10d. on cacao grown in British possessions. From this date it gradually diminished. High duties hampered for many years the sale of cocoa, tea and coffee, but in recent times these duties have been brought down to more reasonable figures. For many years before 1915 the import duty was 1d. per pound on the raw cacao beans, 1d. per pound on cacao butter, and 2s. a hundredweight (less than a farthing a pound) on cacao shells or husks. In the Budget of September, 1915, the above duties were increased by fifty per cent. A further and greater increase was made in the Budget of April, 1916, when cacao was made to pay a higher tax in Britain than in any other country in the world. In 1919 Imperial preference was introduced after a break of over sixty years, the duty on cocoa from foreign countries being 3/4d. a pound more than that from British Possessions.

Duty on Cacao.

1855-1915. 1915. 1916. 1919. Cacao beans per lb. 1d. 1-1/2d. 6d. 4-1/2d. foreign, 3-3/4d. British Cacao butter per lb. 1d. 1-1/2d. 6d. 4-1/2d. foreign, 3-3/4d. British Cacao shells per cwt. 2s. 3s. 12s. 6s. foreign, 5s. British

In considering this duty and its effect on the price of the finished article, it should be remembered that there are substantial losses in manufacture. Thus the beans are cleaned, which removes up to 0.5 per cent.; roasted, which causes a loss by volatilisation of 7 per cent.; and shelled, the husks being about 12 per cent. Therefore, the actual yield of usable nib, which has to bear the whole duty, is about 80 per cent. It may be well to add that the yield of cocoa powder is 48 per cent. of the raw beans, or roughly, one pound of the raw product yields half a pound of the finished article.

Introduction of Cocoa Powder.

The drink "cocoa" as we know it to-day was not introduced until 1828. Before this time the ground bean, mixed with sugar, was sold in cakes. The beverage prepared from these chocolate cakes was very rich in butter, and whilst the British Navy has always consumed it in this condition (the sailors generally remove with a spoon the excess of butter which floats to the top) it is a little heavy for less hardy digestions. Van Houten (of the well-known Dutch house of that name) in 1828 invented a method of pressing out part of the butter, and thus obtained a lighter, more appetising, and more easily assimilated preparation. As the butter is useful in chocolate manufacture, this process enabled the manufacturer to produce a less costly cocoa powder, and thus the circle of consumers was widened. Messrs. Cadbury Bros., of Birmingham, first sold their "cocoa essence" in 1866, and Messrs. Fry and Sons, of Bristol, introduced a pure cocoa by pressing out part of the butter in 1868.

Growing Popularity of Cacao Preparations.

The incidence of import duties did not prevent the continuous increase in the amount of cacao consumed in the British Isles. When Queen Victoria came to the throne the cacao cleared for home consumption was about four or five thousand tons, more than half of which was consumed by the Navy. At the time of Queen Victoria's death it had increased to four times this amount, and by 1915 it had reached nearly fifty thousand tons. (For statistics of consumption, see p. 183).

* * * * *

This brief sketch of the history of cacao owes much to "Cocoa--all about it," by Historicus (the pseudonym of the late Richard Cadbury). This work is out of print, but those who are fortunate enough to be able to consult it will find therein much that is curious and discursive.

[Illustration: ANCIENT MEXICAN DRINKING CUPS (British Museum)]

CHAPTER II

CACAO AND ITS CULTIVATION

O tree, upraised in far-off Mexico!

"*Ode to the Chocolate Tree*," 1664.

How seldom do we think, when we drink a cup of cocoa or eat some morsels of chocolate, that our liking for these delicacies has set minds and bodies at work all the world over! Many types of humanity have contributed to their production. Picture in the mind's eye the graceful coolie in the sun-saturated tropics, moving in the shade, cutting the pods from the cacao tree; the deep-chested sailor helping to load from lighters or surf-boats the precious bags of cacao into the hold of the ocean liner; the skilful workman roasting the beans until they fill the room with a fine aroma; and the girl with dexterous fingers packing the cocoa or fashioning the chocolate in curious, and delicate forms. To the black and brown races, the negroes and the East Indians, we owe a debt for their work on tropical plantations, for the harder manual work would be too arduous for Europeans unused to the heat of those regions.

Climate Necessary.

Cacao can only grow at tropical temperatures, and when shielded from the wind and unimpaired by drought. Enthusiasts, as a hobby, have grown the tree under glass in England; it requires a warmer temperature than either tea or coffee, and only after infinite care can one succeed in getting the tree to flower and bear fruit. The mean temperature in the countries in which it thrives is about 80 degrees F. in the shade, and the average of the maximum temperatures is seldom more than 90 degrees F., or the average of the minimum temperatures less than 70 degrees F. The rainfall can be as low as 45 inches per annum, as in the Gold Coast, or as high as 150 inches, as in Java, provided the fall is uniformly distributed. The ideal spot is the secluded vale, and whilst in Venezuela there are plantations up to 2000 feet above sea level, cacao cannot generally be profitably cultivated above 1000 feet.

Factors of Geographical Distribution.

Climate, soil, and manures determine the possible region of cultivation--the extent to which the area is utilised depends on the enterprise of man. The original home of cacao was the rich tropical region, far-famed in Elizabethan days, that lies between the Amazon and the Orinoco, and but for the enterprise of man it is doubtful if it would have ever spread from this region. Monkeys often carry the beans many miles--man, the master-monkey, has carried them round the world. First the Indians spread cacao over the tropical belt of the American continent and cultivated it as far North as Mexico. Then came the Spanish explorers of the New World, who carried it from the mainland to the adjacent West Indian islands. Cacao was planted by them in Trinidad as early as 1525. Since that date it has been successfully introduced into many a tropical island. It was an important day in the history of Ceylon when Sir R. Horton, in 1834, had cacao plants brought to that island from Trinidad. The carefully packed plants survived the ordeal of a voyage of ten thousand miles. The most recent introduction is, however, the most striking. About 1880 a native of the Gold Coast obtained some beans, probably from Fernando Po. In 1891, the first bag of cacao was exported; it weighed 80 pounds. In 1915, 24 years later, the export from the Gold Coast was 120 million pounds.

[Illustration: CACAO TREE, WITH PODS AND LEAVES]

The Cacao Tree.

Tropical vegetation appears so bizarre to the visitor from temperate climes that in such surroundings the cacao tree seems almost commonplace. It is in appearance as moderate and unpretentious as an apple tree, though somewhat taller, being, when full grown, about twenty feet high. It begins to bear in its fourth or fifth year. Smooth in its early youth, as it gets older it becomes covered with little bosses (cushions) from which many flowers spring. I saw one fellow, very tall and gnarled, and with many pods on it; turning to the planter I enquired "How old is that tree?" He replied, almost reverentially: "It's a good deal older than I am; must be at least fifty years old." "It's one of the tallest cacao trees I've seen. I wonder--." The planter perceived my thought, and said: "I'll have it measured for you." It was forty feet high. That was a tall one; usually they are not more than half that height. The bark is reddish-grey, and may be partly hidden by brown, grey and green patches of lichen. The bark is both beautiful and quaint, but in the main the tree owes its beauty to its luxuriance of prosperous leaves, and its quaintness to its pods.

[Illustration: CACAO TREE, SHOWING PODS GROWING FROM TRUNK.]

[Illustration: FLOWERS AND FRUITS ON MAIN BRANCHES OF A CACAO TREE. (Reproduced from van Hall's *Cocoa*, by permission of Messrs. Macmillan & Co.).]

The Flowers, Leaves and Fruit.

Although cacao trees are not unlike the fruit trees of England, there are differences which, when first one sees them, cause expressions of surprise and pleasure to leap to the lips. One sees what one never saw before, the fruit springing from the main trunk, quite close to the ground. An old writer has explained that this is due to a wise providence, because the pod is so heavy that if it hung from the end of the branches it would fall off before it reached maturity. The old writer talks of providence; a modern writer would see in the same facts a simple example of evolution. On the same cacao tree every day of the year may be found flowers, young podkins and mature pods side by side. I say "found" advisedly--at the first glance one does not see the flowers because they are so dainty and so small. The buds are the size of rice grains, and the flowers are not more than half an inch across when the petals are fully out. The flowers are pink or yellow, of wax-like appearance, and have no odour. They were commonly stated to be pollinated by thrips and other insects. Dr. von Faber of Java has recently shown that whilst self-pollination is the rule, cross fertilisation occurs between the flowers on adjacent or interlocking trees. These graceful flowers are so small that one can walk through a plantation without observing them, although an average tree will produce six thousand blossoms in a year. Not more than one per cent. of these will become fruit. Usually it takes six months for the bud to develop into the mature fruit. The lovely mosses that grow on the stems and branches are sometimes so thick that they have to be destroyed, or the fragile cacao flower could not push its way through. Whilst the flowers are small, the leaves are large, being as an average about a foot in length and four inches in breadth. The cacao tree never appears naked, save on the rare occasions when it is stripped by the wind, and the leaves are green all the year round, save when they are red, if the reader will pardon an Hibernianism. And indeed there is something contrary in the crimson tint, for whilst we usually associate this with old leaves about to fall, with the cacao, as with some rose trees, it is the tint of the young leaves.

[Illustration: CACAO PODS.]

The Cacao Pod.

The fruit, which hangs on a short thick stalk, may be anything in shape from a melon to a stumpy, irregular cucumber, according to the botanic variety. The intermediate shape is like a lemon, with furrows from end to end. There are pods, called Calabacillo, smooth and ovate like a calabash, and there are others, more rare, so "nobbly" that they are well-named "Alligator." The pods vary in length from five to eleven inches, "with here and there the great pod of all, the blood-red *sangre-tora*." The colours of the pods are as brilliant as they are various. They are rich and strong, and resemble those of the rind of the pomegranate. One pod shows many shades of dull crimson, another grades from gold to the yellow of leather, and yet another is all lack-lustre pea-green. They may be likened to Chinese lanterns hanging in the woods. One does not conclude from the appearance of the pod that the contents are edible, any more than one would surmise that tea-leaves could be used to produce a refreshing drink. I say as much to the planter, who smiles. With one deft cut with his machete or cutlass, which hangs in a leather scabbard by his side, the planter severs the pod from the tree, and with another slash cuts the thick, almost woody rind and breaks open the pod. There is disclosed a mass of some thirty or forty beans, covered with juicy pulp. The inside of the rind and the mass of beans are gleaming white, like melting snow. Sometimes the mass is pale amethyst in colour. I perceive a pleasant odour resembling melon. Like little Jack Horner, I put in my thumb and pull out a snow-white bean. It is slippery to hold, so I put it in my mouth. The taste is sweet, something between grape and melon. Inside this fruity coating is the bean proper. From different pods we take beans and cut them in two, and find that the colour of the bean varies from purple almost to white.

[Illustration: CUT POD, REVEALING THE WHITE PULP ROUND THE BEANS (CEYLON.)]

[Illustration: CACAO PODS, SHEWING BEANS INSIDE.]

Botanical Description.

Theobroma Cacao belongs to the family of the *Sterculiaceae*, and to the same order as the Limes and Mallows. It is described in Strasburger's admirable *Text-Book of Botany* as follows:

"Family. *Sterculiaceae.*

IMPORTANT GENERA. The most important plant is the Cocoa Tree (*Theobroma Cacao*). It is a low tree with short-stalked, firm, brittle, simple leaves of large size, oval shape, and dark green colour. The young leaves are of a bright red colour, and, as in many tropical trees, hang limply downwards. The flowers are borne on the main stem or the older branches, and arise from dormant axillary buds (Cauliflory). Each petal is bulged up at the base, narrows considerably above this, and ends in an expanded tip. The form of the reddish flowers is thus somewhat urn-shaped with five radiating points. The pentalocular ovary has numerous ovules in each loculus. As the fruit develops, the soft tissue of the septa extends between the single seeds; the ripe fruit is thus unilocular and many-seeded. The seed-coat is filled by the embryo, which has two large, folded, brittle cotyledons."

The last sentence conveys an erroneous impression. The two cotyledons, which form the seed, are not brittle when found in nature in the pod. They are juicy and fleshy. And it is only after the seed has received special treatment (fermentation and drying) to obtain the bean of commerce, that it becomes brittle.

Varieties of Theobroma Cacao.

As mentioned above, the pods and seeds of Theobroma Cacao trees show a marked variation, and in every country the botanist has studied these variations and classified the trees according to the shape and colour of the pods and seeds. The existence of so many classifications has led to a good deal of confusion, and we are indebted to Van Hall for the simplest way of clearing up these difficulties. He accepts the classification first given by

Morris, dividing the trees into two varieties--Criollo and Forastero:

[Illustration: DRAWINGS OF TYPICAL PODS, illustrating varieties. CRIOLLO FORASTERO FORASTERO (CALABACILLO VARIETY)]

Extremes of Characteristics.

Criollo. Forastero.

(Old Red, Caracas, etc.) Grading from Cundeamor (bottle-necked) to Calabacillo (smooth).

Pod walls. Thin and warty. Thick and woody.

Beans. Large and plump. Small and flat. White. Heliotrope to purple. Sweet. Astringent.

The cacao of the criollo variety has pods the walls of which are thin and warty, with ten distinct furrows. The seeds or beans are white as ivory throughout, round and plump, and sweet to taste. The forastero variety includes many sub-varieties, the kind most distinct from the criollo having pods, the walls of which are thick and woody, the surface smooth, the furrows indistinct, and the shape globular. The seeds in these pods are purple in colour, flat in appearance, and bitter to taste. This is a very convenient classification. Personally I believe it would be possible to find pods varying by almost imperceptible gradations from the finest, purest, criollo to the lowest form of forastero (namely, calabacillo). The criollo yields the finest and rarest kind of cacao, but as sometimes happens with refined types in nature, it is a rather delicate tree, especially liable to canker and bark diseases, and this accounts for the predominance of the forastero in the cacao plantations of the world.

The Cacao Plantation.

One can spend happy days on a cacao estate. "Are you going into the cocoa?" they ask, just as in England we might enquire, "Are you going into the corn?"

[Illustration: TROPICAL FOREST, TRINIDAD. This has to be cleared before planting begins.]

Coconut plantations and sugar estates make a strong appeal to the imagination, but for peaceful beauty they cannot compare with the cacao plantation. True, coconut plantations are very lovely--the palms are so graceful, the leaves against the sky so like a fine etching--but "the slender coco's drooping crown of plumes" is altogether foreign to English eyes. Sugar estates are generally marred by the prosaic factory in the background. They are dead level plains, and the giant grass affords no shade from the relentless sun. Whereas the leaves of the cacao tree are large and numerous, so that even in the heat of the day, it is comparatively cool and pleasant under the cacao.

Cacao plantations present in different countries every variety of appearance--from that of a wild forest in which the greater portion of the trees are cacao, to the tidy and orderly plantation. In some of the Trinidad plantations the trees are planted in parallel lines twelve feet apart, with a tree every twelve feet along the line; and as you push your way through the plantation the apparently irregularly scattered trees are seen to flash momentarily into long lines. In other parts of the world, for example, in Grenada and Surinam, the ground may be kept so tidy and free from weeds that they have the appearance of gardens.

Clearing the Land.

When the planter has chosen a suitable site, an exercise requiring skill, the forest has to be cleared. The felling of great trees and the clearing of the wild tangle of undergrowth is arduous work. It is well to leave the trees on the ridges for about sixty feet on either side, and thus form a belt of trees to act as wind screen. Cacao trees are as sensitive to a draught as some human beings, and these "*wind breaks*" are often deliberately grown--Balata, Poui, Mango (Trinidad), Galba (Grenada), Wild Pois Doux (Martinique), and other leafy trees being suitable for this purpose.

Suitable Soil.

It was for many years believed that if a tree were analysed the best soil for its growth could at once be inferred and described, as it was assumed that the best soil would be one containing the same elements in similar proportions. This simple theory ignored the characteristic powers of assimilation of the tree in question and the "digestibility" of the soil constituents. However, it is agreed that soils rich in potash and lime (e.g., those obtained by the decomposition of certain volcanic rocks) are good for cacao. An open sandy or loamy alluvial soil is considered ideal. The physical condition of the soil is equally important: heavy clays or water-logged soils are bad. The depth of soil required depends on its nature. A stiff soil discourages the growth of the "tap" root, which in good porous soils is generally seven or eight feet long.

[Illustration: CHARACTERISTIC ROOT SYSTEM OF THE CACAO TREE. Note the long tap root. (Reproduced from the Imperial Institute series of Handbooks to the Commercial Resources of the Tropics, by permission.)]

Manure.

The greater part of the world's cacao is produced without the use of artificial manures. The soil, which is continually washed down by the rains into the rivers, is continually renewed by decomposition of the bed rock, and in the tropics this decomposition is more rapid than in temperate climes. In Guayaquil, "notwithstanding the fact that the same soil has been cropped consecutively for over a hundred years, there is as yet no sign of decadence, nor does a necessity yet arise for artificial manure."[1] However, manures are useful with all soils, and necessary with many. Happy is the planter who is so placed that he can obtain a plentiful supply of farmyard or pen manure, as this gives excellent results. "Mulching" is also recommended. This consists of covering the ground with decaying leaves, grasses, etc., which keep the soil in a moist and open condition during the dry season. If artificial manures are used they should vary according to the soil, and, although he can obtain considerable help from the analyst, the planter's most reliable guide will be experiment on the spot.

[1] *Bulletin*, Botanic Dept., Jamaica, February, 1900.

Planting.

In the past insufficient care has been taken in *the selection of seed*. The planter should choose the large plump beans with a pale interior, or he should choose the nearest kind to this that is sufficiently hardy to thrive in the particular environment. He can plant (1) direct from seeds, or (2) from seedlings--plants raised in nurseries in bamboo pots, or (3) by grafting or budding. It is usual to plant two or three seeds in each hole, and destroy the weaker plants when about a foot high. The seeds are planted from twelve to fifteen feet apart. The distance chosen depends chiefly on the richness of the soil; the richer the soil, the more ample room is allowed for the trees to spread without choking each other. Interesting results have been obtained by Hart and others by grafting the fine but tender criollo on to the hardy forastero, but until yesterday the practice had not been tried on a large scale. Experiments were begun in 1913 by Mr. W.G.

Freeman in Trinidad which promise interesting results. By 1919 the Department of Agriculture had seven acres in grafted and budded cacao. In a few years it should be possible to say whether it pays to form an estate of budded cacao in preference to using seedlings.

[Illustration: NURSERY, WITH THE YOUNG CACAO PLANTS IN BASKETS, JAVA. (Reproduced from van Hall's *Cocoa*, by permission of Messrs. Macmillan & Co.).]

[Illustration: PLANTING CACAO, TRINIDAD, FROM YOUNG SEEDLINGS IN BAMBOO POTS.]

[Illustration: CACAO IN ITS FOURTH YEAR (SAMOA).]

There are no longer any mystic rites performed before planting. In the old days it was the custom to solemnize the planting, for example, by sacrificing a cacao-coloured dog (see Bancroft's *Native Races of the Pacific States*.)

Shade: Temporary and Permanent.

[Illustration: COPY OF AN OLD ENGRAVING SHOWING THE CACAO TREE, AND A TREE SHADING IT. (From *Bontekoe's Works*.)]

When the seeds are planted, such small plants as cassava, chillies, pigeon peas and the like are planted with them. The object of planting these is to afford the young cacao plant shelter from the sun, and to keep the ground in good condition. Incidentally the planter obtains cassava (which gives tapioca), red peppers, etc., as a "catch crop" whilst he is waiting for the cacao tree to begin to yield. Bananas and plantains are planted with the same object, and these are allowed to remain for a longer period. Such is the rapidity of plant growth in the tropics that in three or four years the cacao tree is taller than a man, and begins to bear fruit in its fourth or fifth year. Now it is agreed that, as with men, the cacao tree needs protection in its youth, but whether it needs shade trees when it is fully grown is one of the controverted questions. When the planter is sitting after his day's work is done, and no fresh topic comes to his mind, he often re-opens the discussion on the question of shade. The idea that cacao trees need shade is a very ancient one, as is shown in a very old drawing (possibly the oldest drawing of cacao extant) beneath which it is written: "Of the tree which bears cacao, which is money, and how the Indians obtained fire with two pieces of wood." In this drawing you will observe how lovingly the shade tree shelters the cacao. The intention in using shade is to imitate the natural forest conditions in which the wild cacao grew. Sometimes when clearing the forest certain large trees are left standing, but more frequently and with better judgment, chosen kinds are planted. Many trees have been used: the saman, bread fruit, mango, mammet, sand box, pois doux, rubber, etc. In the illustration showing kapok acting as a parasol for cacao in Java, we see that the proportion of shade trees to cacao is high. Leguminous trees are preferred because they conserve the nitrogen in the soil. Hence in Trinidad the favourite shade tree is *Erythrina* or Bois Immortel (so called, a humourist suggests, because it is short-lived). It is also rather prettily named, "Mother of Cacao." Usually the shade trees are planted about 40 feet apart, but there are cacao plantations which might cause a stranger to enquire, "Is this an Immortel plantation?" so closely are these conspicuous trees planted. When looking down a Trinidad valley, richly planted with cacao, one sees in every direction the silver-grey trunks of the Immortel. In the early months of the year these trees have no leaves, they are a mass of flame-coloured flowers, each "shafted like a scimitar." It well repays the labour of climbing a hill to look down on this vermilion glory. Some Trinidad planters believe that their trees would die without shade, yet in Grenada, only a hundred miles North as the steamer sails, there are whole plantations without a single shade tree. The Grenadians say: "You cannot have pods without flowers, and you cannot have good flowering without light and air." Shade trees are not used on some estates in San Thomé, and in Brazil there are cocoa kings with 200,000 trees without one shade tree. It should be mentioned, however, that in these countries the cacao trees are planted more closely (about eight feet apart) and themselves shade the soil. Professor Carmody, in reporting[2] recently on the result of a four years' experiment with (1) shade, (2) no shade, (3) partial shade, says that so far partial shade has given the best results. No general solution has yet been found to the question of the advantage of shade, and, as Shaw states for morality, so in agriculture, "the golden rule is that there is no golden rule." Not only is there the personal factor, but nature provides an infinite variety of environments, and the best results are obtained by the use of methods appropriate to the local conditions.

[2] *Bulletin* Dept. of Agriculture, Trinidad, 1916.

[Illustration: CACAO TREES, SHADED BY KAPOK (*Eriodendron Anfractuosum*) IN JAVA. (reproduced from van Hall's *Cocoa*, by permission of Messrs. Macmillan & Co.)]

[Illustration: CACAO TREES, SHADED BY BOIS IMMORTEL, TRINIDAD.]

Form of Tree-growth Desired: Suckers.

Viscount Mountmorres, in a delightfully clear exposition of cacao cultivation which he gave to the native farmers and chiefs of the Gold Coast in 1906, said: "In pruning, it is necessary always to bear in mind that the best shape for cacao trees is that of an enlarged open umbrella," with a height under the umbrella not exceeding seven feet. With this ideal in his mind, the planter should train up the tree in the way it should go. Viscount Mountmorres also said that everything that grows upwards, except the main stem, must be cut off.

This opens a question which is of great interest to planters as to whether it is wise to allow shoots to grow out from the main trunk near the ground. Some hold that the high yield on their plantation is due to letting these upright shoots grow. "Mi Amigo Corsicano said: 'Diavolo, let the cacao-trees grow, let them branch off like any other fruit-tree, say the tamarind, the 'chupon' or sucker will in time bear more than its mother.'"[3] There seems to be some evidence that *old* trees profit from the "chupons" because they continue to bear when the old trunk is weary, but this is compensated for by the fact that the "chupons" (Portuguese for suckers) were grown at the expense of the tree in its youth. Hence other planters call them "thieves," and "gormandizers," saying that they suck the sap from the tree, turning all to wood. They follow the advice given as early as 1730 by the author of *The Natural History of Chocolate*, when he says: "Cut or lop off the suckers." In Trinidad, experiments have been started, and after a five years' test, Professor Carmody says that the indications are that it is a matter of indifference whether "chupons" are allowed to grow or not.

[3] "*How José formed his Cocoa Estate.*"

[Illustration: CACAO TREE, WITH SUCKERS, TRINIDAD.]

After hunting, agriculture is man's oldest industry, and improvements come but slowly, for the proving of a theory often requires work on a huge scale carried out for several decades. The husbandry of the earth goes on from century to century with little change, and the methods followed are the winnowings of experience, tempered with indolence. And even with the bewildering progress of science in other directions, sound improvements in this field are rare discoveries. There is great scope for the application of physical and chemical knowledge to the production of the raw materials of the tropics. In one or two instances notable advances have been made, thus the direct production of a white sugar (as now practised at Java) at the tropical factory will have far-reaching effects, but with many tropical products the methods practised are as ancient as they are haphazard. Like all methods founded on long experience, they suit the environment and the temperament of the people who use them, so that the work of the scientist in introducing improvements requires intimate knowledge of the conditions if his suggestions are to be adopted. The various Departments of Agriculture are doing splendid pioneer work, but the full harvest of their sowing will not be reaped until the number of tropically-educated agriculturists has been increased by the founding of three or four agricultural colleges and research laboratories in equatorial regions.

There is much research to be done. As yet, however, many planters are ignorant of all that is already established, the facilities for education in tropical agriculture being few and far between. There are signs, however, of development in this direction. It is pleasant to note that a start was made in Ceylon at the end of 1917 by opening an agricultural school at Peradenija. Trinidad has for a number of years had an agricultural school, and is eager to have a college devoted to agriculture. In 1919, Messrs. Cadbury Bros. gave £5000 to form the nucleus of a special educational fund for the Gold Coast. The scientists attached to the several government agricultural departments in Java, Ceylon, Trinidad, the Philippines, Africa, etc., have done splendid work, but it is desirable that the number of workers should be increased. When the world wakes up to the importance of tropical produce, agricultural colleges will be scattered about the tropics, so that every would-be planter can learn his subject on the spot.

[Illustration: CUTLASSING.]

Diseases of the Cacao Tree.

Take, for example, the case of the diseases of plants. Everyone who takes an interest in the garden knows how destructive the insect pests and vegetable parasites can be. In the tropics their power for destruction is very great, and they are a constant menace to economic products like cacao. The importance of understanding their habits, and of studying methods of keeping them in check, is readily appreciated; the planter may be ruined by lacking this knowledge.

The cacao tree has been improved and "domesticated" to satisfy human requirements, a process which has rendered it weaker to resist attacks from pests and parasites. It is usual to classify man amongst the pests, as either from ignorance or by careless handling he can do the tree much harm. Other animal pests are the wanton thieves: monkeys, squirrels and rats, who destroy more fruit than they consume. The insect pests include varieties of beetles, thrips, aphides, scale insects and ants, whilst fungi are the cause of the "Canker" in the stem and branches, the "Witch-broom" disease in twigs and leaves, and the "Black Rot" of pods.

The subject is too immense to be summarised in a few lines, and I recommend readers who wish to know more of this or other division of the science of cacao cultivation, to consult one or more of the four classics in English on this subject:

Cocoa, by Herbert Wright (Ceylon), 1907. *Cacao*, by J. Hinchley Hart (Trinidad), 1911. *Cocoa*, by W.H. Johnson (Nigeria), 1912. *Cocoa*, by C.J.J. van Hall (Java), 1914.

CHAPTER III

HARVESTING AND PREPARATION FOR THE MARKET

The picking, gathering, and breaking of the cacao are the easiest jobs on the plantation.

"How José formed his Cocoa Estate."

Gathering and Heaping.

[Illustration]

In the last chapter I gave a brief account of the cultivation of cacao. I did not deal with forking, spraying, cutlassing, weeding, and so forth, as it would lead us too far into purely technical discussions. I propose we assume that the planter has managed his estate well, and that the plantation is before us looking very healthy and full of fruit waiting to be picked. The question arises: How shall we gather it? Shall we shake the tree? Cacao pods do not fall off the tree even when over-ripe. Shall we knock off or pluck the pods? To do so would make a scar on the trunk of the tree, and these wounds are dangerous in tropical climates, as they are often attacked by canker. A sharp machete or cutlass is used to cut off the pods which grow on the lower part of the trunk. As the tree is not often strong enough to bear a man, climbing is out of the question, and a knife on a pole is used for cutting off the pods on the upper branches. Various shaped knives are used by different planters, a common and efficient kind (see drawing), resembles a hand of steel, with the thumb as a hook, so that the pod-stalk can be cut either by a push or a pull. A good deal of ingenuity has been expended in devising a "foolproof" picker which shall render easy the cutting of the pod-stalk and yet not cut or damage the bark of the tree. A good example is the Agostini picker, which was approved by Hart.

[Illustration: (1) COMMON TYPE OF CACAO PICKER. (2) AGOSTINI CACAO PICKER.]

The gathering of the fruits of one's labour is a pleasant task, which occurs generally only at rare intervals. Cacao is gathered the whole year round. There is, however, in most districts one principal harvest period, and a subsidiary harvest.

[Illustration: GATHERING CACAO PODS, TRINIDAD.]

With cacao in the tropics, as with corn in England, the gathering of the harvest is a delight to lovers of the beautiful. It is a great charm of the cacao plantation that the trees are so closely planted that nowhere does the sunlight find between the foliage a space larger than a man's hand. After the universal glare outside, it seems dark under the cacao, although the ground is bright with dappled sunshine. You hear a noise of talking, of rustling leaves, and falling pods. You come upon a band of coolies or negroes. One near you carries a long bamboo--as long as a fishing rod--with a knife at the end. With a lithe movement he inserts it between the boughs, and, by giving it a sharp jerk, neatly cuts the stalk of a pod, which falls from the tree to the ground. Only the ripe pods must be picked. To do this, not only must the picker's aim be true, but he must also have a good eye for colour. Whether the pods be red or green, as soon as the colour begins to be tinted with yellow it is ripe for picking. This change occurs first along the furrows in the pod. Fewer unripe pods would be gathered if only one kind of pod were grown on one plantation. The confusion of kinds and colours which is often found makes sound judgment very difficult. That the men generally judge correctly the ripeness of pods high in the trees is something to wonder at. The pickers pass on, strewing the earth with ripe pods. They are followed by the graceful, dark-skinned girls, who gather one by one the fallen pods from the greenery, until their baskets are full. Sometimes a basketful is too heavy and the girl cannot comfortably lift it on to her head, but when one of the men has helped her to place it there, she carries it lightly enough. She trips through the trees, her bracelets jingling, and tumbles the pods on to the heap. Once one has seen a great heap of cacao pods it glows in one's memory: anything more rich, more daring in the way of colour one's eye is unlikely to light on. The artist, seeking only an æsthetic effect would be content with this for the consummation and would wish the pods to remain unbroken.

[Illustration: COLLECTING CACAO PODS INTO A HEAP PRIOR TO BREAKING.]

Breaking and Extracting.

There are planters who believe that the product is improved by leaving the gathered pods several days before breaking; and they would follow the practice, but for the risk of losses by theft. Hence the pods are generally broken on the same day as they are gathered. The primitive methods of breaking with a club or by banging on a hard surface are happily little used. Masson of New York made pod-breaking machines, and Sir George Watt has recently invented an ingenious machine for squeezing the beans out of the pod, but at present the extraction is done almost universally by hand, either by men or women. A knife which would cut the husk of the pod and was so constructed that it could not injure the beans within, would be a useful invention. The human extractor has the advantage that he or she can distinguish the diseased, unripe or germinated beans and separate them from the good ones. Picture the men sitting round the heap of pods and, farther out, in a larger circle, twice as many girls with baskets. The man breaks the pod and the girls extract the beans. The man takes the pod in his left hand and gives it a sharp slash with a small cutlass, just cutting through the tough shell of the pod, but not into the beans inside; and then gives the blade, which he has embedded in the shell, a twisting jerk, so that the pod breaks in two with a crisp crack. The girls take the broken pods and scoop out the snow-like beans with a flat wooden spoon or a piece of rib-bone, the beans being pulled off the stringy core (or placenta) which holds them together. The beans are put preferably into baskets or, failing these, on to broad banana leaves, which are used as trays.

Practice renders these processes cheerful and easy work, often performed to an accompaniment of laughing and chattering.

[Illustration: MEN BREAKING PODS, GIRLS SCOOPING OUT BEANS, AND MULES WAITING WITH BASKETS TO CONVEY THE CACAO TO THE FERMENTARY.]

Fermenting.

I allow myself the pleasure of thinking that I am causing some of my readers a little surprise when I tell them that cacao is fermented, and that the fermentation produces alcohol. As I mentioned above, the cacao bean is covered with a fruity pulp. The bean as it comes from the pod is moist, whilst the pulp is full of juice. It would be impossible to convey it to Europe in this condition; it would decompose, and, when it reached its destination, would be worthless. In order that a product can be handled commercially it is desirable to have it in such a condition that it does not change, and thus with cacao it becomes necessary to get rid of the pulp, and, whilst this may be done by washing or simply by drying, experience has shown that the finest and driest product is obtained when the drying is preceded by fermentation. Just as broken grapes will ferment, so will the fruity pulp of the cacao bean. Present day fermentaries are simply convenient places for storing the cacao whilst the process goes on. In the process of fermentation, Dr. Chittenden says the beans are "stewed in their own juice." This may be expressed less picturesquely but more accurately by saying the beans are warmed by the heat of their own fermenting pulp, from which they absorb liquid.

In Trinidad the cacao which the girls have scooped out into the baskets is emptied into larger baskets, two of which are "crooked" on a mule's back, and carried thus to the fermentary. In Surinam it is conveyed by boat, and in San Thomé by trucks, which run on Decauville railways.

The period of fermentation and the receptacle to hold the cacao vary from country to country. With cacao of the criollo type only one or two days fermentation is required, and as a result, in Ecuador and Ceylon, the cacao is simply put in heaps on a suitable floor. In Trinidad and the majority of other cacao-producing areas, where the forastero variety predominates, from five to nine days are required. The cacao is put into the "sweat" boxes and covered with banana or plantain leaves to keep in the heat. The boxes may measure four feet each way and be made of sweet-smelling cedar wood. As is usual with fermentation, the temperature begins to rise, and if you thrust your hands into the fermenting beans you find they are as hot and mucilaginous as a poultice.

[Illustration: "SWEATING" BOXES, TRINIDAD. The man is holding the wooden spade used for turning the beans.]

Time. Temperature. When put in 25° C. or 77° F. After 1 day 30° C. or 89° F. After 2 days 37° C. or 98° F. After 3 days 47° C. or 115° F.

(After the third day the heat is maintained, but the temperature rises very little.)

The temperature is the simplest guide to the amount of fermentation taking place, and the uniformity of the temperature in all parts of the mass is desirable, as showing that all parts are fermenting evenly. The cacao is usually shovelled from one box to another every one or two days. The chief object of this operation is to mix the cacao and prevent merely local fermentation. To make mixing easy one ingenious planter uses a cylindrical vessel which can be turned about on its axis.

[Illustration: FERMENTING BOXES, JAVA. From the last box the beans are shovelled into the washing basin. (Reproduced from van Hall's *Cocoa*, by permission of Messrs. Macmillan & Co.)]

In other places, for example in Java, the boxes are arranged as a series of steps, so that the cacao is transferred with little labour from the higher to the lower. In San Thomé the cacao is placed on the plantation direct into trucks, which are covered with plaintain leaves, and run on rails through the plantation right into the fermentary. Some day some enterprising firm will build a fermentary in portable sections easily erected, and with some simple mechanical mixer to replace the present laborious method of turning the beans by manual labour.

The general conditions[1] for a good fermentation are:

(1) The mass of beans must be kept warm.

(2) The mass of beans must be moist, but not sodden.

(3) In the later stages there must be sufficient air.

(4) The boxes must be kept clean.

[1] For full details see the pamphlet by the author on *The Practice of Fermentation in Trinidad*.

Changes during Fermentation.

No entirely satisfactory theory of the changes in cacao due to fermentation has yet been established. It is known that the sugary pulp outside the beans ferments in a similar way to other fruit pulp, save that for a yeast fermentation the temperature rises unusually high (in three days to 47 degrees C.), and also that there are parallel and more important changes in the interior of the bean. The difficulty of establishing a complete theory of fermentation of cacao has not daunted the scientists, for they know that the roses of philosophy are gathered by just those who can grasp the thorniest problems. Success, however, is so far only partial, as can be seen by consulting the best introduction on the subject, the admirable collection of essays on *The Fermentation of Cacao*, edited by H. Hamel Smith. Here the reader will find the valuable contributions of Fickendey, Loew, Nicholls, Preyer, Schulte im Hofe, and Sack.

The obvious changes which occur in the breaking down of the fruity exterior of the bean should be carefully distinguished from the subtle changes in the bean itself. Let us consider them separately:--

(*a*) *Changes in the Pulp.*--Just as grape-pulp ferments and changes to wine, and just as weak wine if left exposed becomes sour; so the fruity sugary pulp outside the cacao bean on exposure gives off bubbles of carbon dioxide, becomes alcoholic, and later becomes acid. The acid produced is generally the pleasant vinegar acid (acetic acid), but under some circumstances it may be lactic acid, or the rancid-smelling butyric acid. Kismet! The planter trusts to nature to provide the right kind of fermentation. This fermentation is set up and carried on by the minute organisms (yeasts, bacteria, etc.), which chance to fall on the beans from the air or come from the sides of the receptacle. One yeast-cell does not make a fermentation, and as no yeast is added a day is wasted whilst any yeasts which happen to be present are multiplying to an army large enough to produce a visible effect on the pulp. *Any* organism which happens to be on the pod, in the air, or on the inside of the fermentary will multiply in the pulp, if the pulp contains suitable nourishment. Each kind of organism produces its own characteristic changes. It would thus appear a miracle if the same substances were always produced. Yet, just as grape-juice left exposed to every micro-organism of the air, generally changes in the direction of wine more or less good, so the pulp of cacao tends, broadly speaking, to ferment in one way. It would, however, be a serious error to assume that exactly the same kind of fermentation takes place in any two fermentaries in the world, and the maximum variation must be considerable. As the pulp ferments, it is destroyed; it gradually changes from white to brown, and a liquid ("sweatings") flows away from it. The "*sweatings*" taste like sweet cider. At present this is allowed to run away through holes in the bottom of the box, and no care is taken to preserve what may yet become a valuable by-product. I found by experiment that in the preparation of one cwt. of dry beans about 1-1/2 gallons of this unstable liquid are produced. In other words, some seven or eight million gallons of "sweatings" run to waste every year. In most cases only small quantities are produced in one place at one time. This, and the lack of knowledge of scientifically controlled fermentation, and the difficulty of bottling, prevent the starting of an industry producing either a new drink or a vinegar. The cacao juice or "sweatings" contains about fifteen per cent. of solids, about half of which consists of sugars. If the fermentation of the cacao were centralised in the various districts, and conducted on a large scale under a chemist's control, the sugars could be obtained, or an alcoholic liquid or a vinegar could easily be prepared.

[Illustration: CHARGING THE CACAO ON TO TRUCKS IN THE PLANTATION, SAN THOMÉ.]

[Illustration: CACAO IN THE FERMENTING TRUCKS, SAN THOMÉ. The covering of banana leaves keeps the beans warm.]

The planter decides when the beans are fermented by simply looking at them; he judges their condition by the colour of the pulp. When they are ready to be removed from the fermentary they are plump, and brown without, and juicy within.

(*b*) *Changes in the Interior of the Bean.*--What is the relation between the comparatively simple fermentation of the pulp and the changes in the interior of the bean? This important question has not yet been answered, although a number of attempts have been made.

As far as is known, the living ferments (micro-organisms) do not penetrate the skin of the bean, so that any fermentation which takes place must be promoted by unorganised ferments (or enzymes). Mr. H.C. Brill[2] found raffinase, invertase, casease and protease in the pulp; oxidase, raffinase, casease and emulsinlike enzymes in the fresh bean; and all these six, together with diastase, in the fermented bean. Dr. Fickendey says: "The object of fermentation is, in the main, to kill the germ of the bean in such a manner that the efficiency of the unorganised ferment is in no way impaired."

[2] *Philippine Journal of Science*, 1917.

From my own observations I believe that forastero beans are killed at 47 degrees C. (which is commonly reached when they have been fermenting 60 hours), for a remarkable change takes place at this temperature and time. Whilst the micro-organisms remain outside, the juice of the pulp appears to penetrate not only the skin, but the flesh of the bean, and the brilliant violet in the isolated pigment cells becomes diffused more or less evenly throughout the entire bean, including the "germ." It is certain that the bean absorbs liquid from the outside, for it becomes so plump that its skin is stretched to the utmost. The following changes occur:

(1) *Taste.* An astringent colourless substance (a tannin or a body possessing many properties of a tannin) changes to a tasteless brown substance. The bean begins to taste less astringent as the "tannin" is destroyed. With white (criollo) beans this change is sufficiently advanced in two days, but with purple (forastero)

beans it may take seven days.

(2) *Colour.* The change in the tannin results in the white (criollo) beans becoming brown and the purple (forastero) beans becoming tinged with brown. The action resembles the browning of a freshly-cut apple, and has been shown to be due to oxygen (activated by an oxidase, a ferment encouraging combination with oxygen) acting on the astringent colourless substance, which, like the photographic developer, pyrogallic acid, becomes brown on oxidation.

(3) *Aroma.* A notable change is that substances are created within the bean, which *on roasting* produce the fine aromatic odour characteristic of cocoa and chocolate, and which Messrs. Bainbridge and Davies have shown is due to a trace (0.001 per cent.) of an essential oil over half of which consists of linalool.[3]

(4) *Stimulating Effect.* It is commonly stated that during fermentation there is generated theobromine, the alkaloid which gives cacao its stimulating properties, but the estimation of theobromine in fermented and unfermented beans does not support this.

(5) *Consistency.* Fermented beans become crisp on drying. This development may be due to the "tannins" encountering, in their dispersion through the bean, proteins, which are thus converted into bodies which are brittle solids on drying (compare tanning of hides). The "hide" of the bean may be similarly "tanned"--the shell certainly becomes leathery (unless washed)--but a far more probable explanation, in both cases, is that the gummy bodies in bean and shell set hard on drying.

[3] *Journal of the Chemical Society*, 1912.

We see, then, that although fermentation was probably originally followed as the best method of getting rid of the pulp, it has other effects which are entirely good. It enables the planter to produce a drier bean, and one which has, when roasted, a finer flavour, colour, and aroma, than the unfermented. Fermentation is generally considered to produce so many desirable results that M. Perrot's suggestion[4] of removing the pulp by treatment with alkali, and thus avoiding fermentation, has not been enthusiastically received.

[4] *Comptes Rendus*, 1913.

Beans which have been dried direct and those which have been fermented may be distinguished as follows:

CACAO BEANS

DRIED DIRECT. FERMENTED AND DRIED.

Shape of bean Flat Plumper *Shell* Soft and close fitting Crisp and more or less free. *Interior: colour* Slate-blue or mud-brown Bright browns and purples " *consistence* Leather to cheese Crisp " *appearance* Solid Open-grained " *taste* More or less bitter Less astringent or astringent

Whilst several effects of fermentation have not been satisfactorily accounted for, I think all are agreed that to obtain one of the chief effects of fermentation, namely the brown colour, oxidation is necessary. All recognise that for this oxidation the presence of three substances is essential:

(1) The tannin to be oxidised.

(2) Oxygen.

(3) An enzyme which encourages the oxidation.

All these occur in the cacao bean as it comes from the pod, but why oxidation occurs so much better in a fermented bean than in a bean which is simply dried is not very clear. If you cut an apple it goes brown owing to the action of oxygen absorbed from the air, but as long as the apple is uncut and unbruised it remains white. If you take a cacao bean from the pod and cut it, the exposed surface goes brown, but if you ferment the bean the whole of it gradually goes brown without being cut. My observations lead me to believe that the bean does not become oxidised until it is killed, that is, until it is no longer capable of germination. It can be killed by raising the temperature, by fermentation or otherwise, or as Dr. Fickendey has shown, by cooling to almost freezing temperatures. It may be that killing the bean makes its skin and cell walls more permeable to oxygen, but my theory is that when the bean is killed disintegration or weakening of the cell walls, etc., occurs, and, as a result, the enzyme and tannin, *hitherto separate*, become mixed, and hence able actively to absorb oxygen. The action of oxygen on the tannin also accounts for the loss of astringency on fermentation, and it may be well to point out that fermentation increases the internal surface of the bean exposed to air and oxygen. The bean, during fermentation, actually sucks in liquid from the surrounding pulp and becomes plumper and fuller. On drying, however, the skin, which has been expanded to its utmost, wrinkles up as the interior contracts and no longer fits tightly to the bean, and the cotyledons having been thrust apart by the liquid, no longer hold together so closely. This accounts for the open appearance of a fermented bean. As on drying large interspaces are produced, these allow the air to circulate more freely and expose a greater surface of the bean to the action of oxygen. Since the liquids in all living matter presumably contain some dissolved oxygen, the problem is to account for the fact that the tannin in the unfermented bean remains unoxidised, whilst that in the fermented bean is easily oxidised. The above affords a partial explanation, and seems fairly satisfactory when taken with my previous suggestion, namely, that during fermentation the bean is rendered pervious to water, which, on distributing itself throughout the bean, dissolves the isolated masses of tannin and diffuses it evenly, so that it encounters and becomes mixed with the enzymes. From this it will be evident that the major part of the oxidation of the tannin occurs during drying, and hence the importance of this, both from the point of view of the keeping properties of the cacao, and its colour, taste and aroma.

It will be realised from the above that there is still a vast amount of work to be done before the chemist will be in a position to obtain the more desirable aromas and flavours. Having found the necessary conditions, scientifically trained overseers will be required to produce them, and for this they will need to have under their direction arrangements for fermentation designed on correct principles and allowing some degree of control. Whilst improvements are always possible in the approach to perfection, it must be admitted that, considering the means at their disposal, the planters produce a remarkably fine product.

[Illustration: FOR DRYING SMALL QUANTITIES. A simple tray-barrow, which can be run under the house when rain comes on.]

Loss on Fermenting and Drying.

The fermented cacao is conveyed from the fermentary to the drying trays or floors. The planter often has some rough check-weighing system. Thus, for example, he notes the number of standard baskets of wet cacao put into the fermentary, and he measures the fermented cacao produced with the help of a bottomless barrel. By this means he finds that on fermentation the beans lose weight by the draining away of the "sweatings," according to the amount and juiciness of the pulp round them. The beans are still very wet, and on drying lose a high percentage of their moisture by evaporation before the cacao bean of commerce is obtained.

The average losses may be tabulated thus:

Weight of wet cacao from pod 100 Loss on fermentation 20 to 25 Loss on drying 40 -------- Cacao beans of commerce obtained 35 to 40

[Illustration: SPREADING THE CACAO BEANS ON MATS TO DRY IN THE SUN, CEYLON.]

The drying of cacao is an art. On the one hand it is necessary to get the beans quite dry (that is, in a condition in which they hold only their normal amount of water--5 to 7 per cent.) or they will be liable to go mouldy. On the other hand, the husk or shell of the bean must not be allowed to become burned or brittle. Brittle shells produce waste in packing and handling, and broken shells allow grubs and mould to enter the beans when the cacao is stored. The method of drying varies in different countries according to the climate. José says: "In the wet season when 'Father Sol' chooses to lie low behind the clouds for days and your cocoa house is full, your curing house full, your trees loaded, then is the time to put on his mettle the energetic and practical planter. In such tight corners, *amigo*, I have known a friend to set a fire under his cocoa house to keep the cocoa on the top somewhat warm. Another friend's plan (and he recommended it) was to address his patron saint on such occasions. He never addressed that saint at other times."

[Illustration: DRYING TRAYS, GRENADA. The trays slide on rails. The corrugated iron roofs will slide over the whole to protect from rain.]

In most producing areas sun-drying is preferred, but in countries where much rain falls, artificial dryers are slowly but surely coming into vogue. These vary in pattern from simple heated rooms, with shelves, to vacuum stoves and revolving drums. The sellers of these machines will agree with me when I say that every progressive planter ought to have one of these artificial aids to use during those depressing periods when the rain continually streams from the sky. On fine days it is difficult to prevent mildew appearing on the cacao, but at such times it is impossible. However, whenever available, the sun's heat is preferable, for it encourages a slow and even drying, which lasts over a period of about three days. As Dr. Paul Preuss says: "Il faut éviter une dessiccation trop rapide. Le cacao ne peut être séché en moins de trois jours."[5] Further, most observers agree with Dr. Sack that the valuable changes, which occur during fermentation, continue during drying, especially those in which oxygen assists. The full advantage of these is lost if the temperature used is high enough to kill the enzymes, or if the drying is too rapid, both of which may occur with artificial drying.

[5] Dr. Paul Preuss, *Le cacao. Culture et Préparation.*

Sun-drying is done on cement or brick floors, on coir mats or trays, or on wooden platforms. In order to dry the cacao uniformly it is raked over and over in the sun. It must be tenderly treated, carefully "watched and caressed," until the interior becomes quite crisp and in colour a beautiful brown.

Sometimes the platforms are built on the top of the fermentaries, the cacao being conveyed through a hole in the roof of the fermentary to the drying platform.

[Illustration: "HAMEL-SMITH" ROTARY DRYER. (Made by Messrs. David Bridge and Co., Manchester).

The receiving cylinders, six in number, are filled approximately three-quarters full with the cacao to be dried. These are then placed in position on the revolving framework, which is enclosed in the casing and slowly revolved. The cylinders are fitted with baffle plates, which gently turn over the cacao beans at each revolution so that even drying throughout is the result. The casing is heated to the requisite temperature by means of a special stove, the arrangement of which is such as to allow the air drawn from the outside to circulate around the stove and to pass into the interior of the casing containing the drying cylinders. The fumes from the fuel do not in any way come in contact with the material during drying.]

[Illustration: DRYING PLATFORMS, TRINIDAD, WITH SLIDING ROOFS.]

In Trinidad the platform always has a sliding roof, which can be pulled over the cacao in the blaze of noon or when a rainstorm comes on. In other places, sliding platforms are used which can be pushed under cover in wet weather.

The Washing of Cacao.

In Java, Ceylon and Madagascar before the cacao is dried, it is first washed to remove all traces of pulp. This removal of pulp enables the beans to be more rapidly dried, and is considered almost a necessity in Ceylon, where sun-drying is difficult. The practice appears at first sight wholly good and sanitary, but although beans so treated have a very clean and bright appearance, looking not unlike almonds, the practice cannot be recommended. There is a loss of from 2 to 10 per cent. in weight, which is a disadvantage to the planter, whilst from the manufacturer's point of view, washing is objectionable because, according to Dr. Paul Preuss, the aroma suffers. Whilst this may be questioned, there is no doubt that washing renders the shells more brittle and friable, and less able to bear carriage and handling; and when the shell is broken, the cacao is more liable to attack by grubs and mould. Therein lies the chief danger of washing.

[Illustration: CACAO DRYING PLATFORMS, SAN THOMÉ. Three tiers of trays on rails. (Reproduced by permission from the Imperial Institute series of Handbooks to the Commercial Resources of the Tropics).]

[Illustration: WASHING THE BEANS IN A VAT TO CLEAN OFF THE PULP, CEYLON.]

Claying, Colouring, and Polishing Cacao.

[Illustration: CLAYING CACAO BEANS IN TRINIDAD.]

Just as in Java and Ceylon, to assist drying, they wash off the pulp, so in Venezuela and often in Trinidad, with the same object, they put earth or clay on the beans. In Venezuela it is a heavy, rough coat, and in Trinidad a film so thin that usually it is not visible. In Venezuela, where fermentation is often only allowed to proceed for one day, the use of fine red earth may possibly be of value. It certainly gives the beans a very pretty appearance; they look as though they have been moistened and rolled in cocoa powder. But in Trinidad, where the fermentation is a lengthy one, the use of clay, though hallowed by custom, is quite unnecessary. In the report of the Commission of Enquiry (Trinidad, 1915) we read concerning claying that "It is said to prevent the bean from becoming mouldy in wet weather, to improve its marketable value by giving it a bright and uniform appearance, and to help to preserve its aroma." In the appendix to this report the following recommendation occurs: "The claying of cacao ought to be avoided as much as possible, and when necessary only sufficient to give a uniform colour ought to be used." In my opinion manufacturers would do well to discourage entirely the claying of cacao either in Trinidad or Venezuela, for from their point of view it has nothing to recommend it. One per cent. of clay is sufficient to give a uniform colour, but occasionally considerably more than this is used. If we are to believe reports, deliberate adulteration is sometimes practised.

Thus in *How José formed his Cocoa Estate* we read: "A cocoa dealer of our day to give a uniform colour to the miscellaneous brands he has purchased from Pedro, Dick, or Sammy will wash the beans in a heap, with a mixture of starch, sour oranges, gum arabic and red ochre. This mixture is always boiled. I can recommend the 'Chinos' in this dodge, who are all adepts in all sorts of 'adulteration' schemes. They even add some grease to this mixture so as to give the beans that brilliant gloss which you see sometimes." In Trinidad the usual way of obtaining a gloss is by the curious operation known as "dancing," which is performed on the moistened beans after the clay has been sprinkled on them. It is a quaint sight to see a circle of seven or eight coloured folk slowly treading a heap of beans. The dancing may proceed for any period up to an hour, and as they tread they sing some weird native chant. Somewhat impressed, I remarked to the planter that it had all the appearance of an incantation. He replied that the process cost 2d. per cwt. Dancing makes the beans look smooth, shiny, and even, and it separates any beans that may be stuck together in clusters. It may make the beans rounder, and it is said to improve their keeping properties, but this remains to be proved. On the whole, if it is considered desirable to produce a glossy appearance, it is better to use a polishing machine.

The Weight of the Cured Cacao Bean.

[Illustration: SORTING CACAO BEANS IN JAVA. (Reproduced from van Hall's *Cocoa*, by permission of Messrs. Macmillan & Co.).]

Planters and others may be interested to know the comparative sizes of the beans from the various producing areas of the world. Some idea of these can be gained by considering the relative weights of the beans as purchased in England.

Average weight Number of Beans Kind. of one Bean. to the lb.

Grenada 1.0 grammes 450 Parâ 1.0 " 450 Bahia 1.1 " 410 Accra 1.2 " 380 Trinidad 1.2 " 380 Cameroons 1.2 " 380 Ceylon 1.2 " 380 Caracas 1.3 " 350 Machala 1.4 " 330 Arriba 1.5 " 300 Carupano 1.6 " 280

The Yield of the Cacao Tree.

The average yield of cacao has in the past generally been over-stated. Whether this is because the planter is an optimist or because he wishes others to think his efforts are crowned with exceptional success, or because he takes a simple pride in his district, is hard to tell. Probably the tendency has been to take the finer estates and put their results down as the average.

Of the thousands of flowers that bloom on one tree during the year, on an average only about twenty develop into mature pods, and each pod yields about 1-1/3 ounces of dry cured cacao. Taking the healthy trees with the neglected, the average yield is from 1-1/2 to 2 pounds of commercial cacao per tree. This seems very small, and those who hear it for the first time often make a rapid mental calculation of the amazing number of trees that must be needed to produce the world's supply, at least 250 million trees. Or again, taking the average yield per acre as 400 lbs., we find that there must be well over a million acres under cacao cultivation. At the Government station at Aburi (Gold Coast) three plots of cacao gave in 1914 an average yield of over 8 pounds of cacao per tree, and in 1918 some 468 trees (*Amelonado*) gave as an average 7.8 pounds per tree. This suggests what might be done by thorough cultivation. It suggests a great opportunity for the planters--that, without planting one more tree, they might quadruple the world's production.

The work which has been started by the Agricultural Department in Trinidad of recording the yield of individual trees has shown that great differences occur. Further, it has generally been observed that the heavy bearing trees of the first year have continued to be heavy bearers, and the poor-yielding trees have remained poor during subsequent years. The report rightly concludes that: "The question of detecting the poor-bearing trees on an estate and having them replaced by trees raised from selected stock, or budded or grafted trees, of known prolific and other good qualities is deserving of the most serious consideration by planters."

The Kind of Cacao that Manufacturers Like.[6]

[6] For further information read *The Qualities in Cacao Desired by Manufacturers*, by N.P. Booth and A.W. Knapp, International Congress of Tropical Agriculture, 1914.

Planters have suggested to me that if the users and producers of cacao could be brought together it would be to their mutual advantage. Permit me to conceive a meeting and report an imaginary conversation:

PLANTER: You know we planters work a little in the dark. We don't know quite what to strive after. Tell me exactly what kind of cacao the manufacturers want?

MANUFACTURER: Every buyer and manufacturer has his tastes and preferences and----.

PLANTER: Don't hedge!

MANUFACTURER: The cacao of each producing area has its special characters, even as the wine from a country, and part of the good manufacturer's art is the art of blending.

PLANTER: What--good with bad?

MANUFACTURER: No! Good of one type with good of another type.

PLANTER: What do you mean exactly by good?

MANUFACTURER: By good I mean large, ripe, well-cured beans. By indifferent I mean unripe and unfermented. By abominable I mean germinated, mouldy, and grubby beans. Happily, the last class is quite a small one.

PLANTER: You don't mean to tell me that only the good cacao sells?

MANUFACTURER: Unfortunately, no! There are users of inferior beans. Practically all the cacao produced--good and indifferent--is bought by someone. Most manufacturers prefer the fine, healthy, well fermented kinds.

PLANTER: Well fermented! They have a strange way of showing their preference. Why, they often pay more for Guayaquil than they do for Grenada cacao. Yet Guayaquil is never properly fermented, whilst that from the Grenada estates is perfectly fermented.

MANUFACTURER: Agreed. Just as you would pay more for a badly-trained thoroughbred than for a well-trained mongrel. It's breed they pay for. The Guayaquil breed is peculiar; there is nothing else like it in the world. You might think the tree had been grafted on to a spice tree. It has a fine characteristic aroma, which is so powerful that it masks the presence of a high percentage of unfermented beans. However, if Guayaquil cacao was well-fermented it would (subject to the iron laws of Supply and Demand) fetch a still higher price, and there would not be the loss there is in a wet season when the Guayaquil cacao, being unfermented, goes mouldy. I think in Grenada they plant for high yield, and not for quality, for the bean is small and approaches the inferior Calabacillo breed. Its value is maintained by an amazing evenness and an uniform excellence in curing. The way in which it is prepared for the market does great credit to the planters.

PLANTER: They don't clay there, do they?

MANUFACTURER: No! and yet it is practically impossible to find a mouldy bean in Grenada estates cacao. Evidently claying is not a necessity--in Grenada.

PLANTER: Ha! ha! By that I suppose you insinuate that it is not a necessity in Trinidad, where the curing is also excellent. Or in Venezuela? What's the buyer's objection to claying?

MANUFACTURER: Simply that claying is camouflage. Actually the buyer doesn't mind so long as the clay is not too generously used. He objects to paying for beans and getting clay. However, it's really too bad to colour up with clay the black cacao from diseased pods; it might deceive even experienced brokers.

PLANTER: Ha! ha! Then it's a very sinful practice. I don't think that ever gets beyond the local tropical market. I know the merchants judge largely by "the skin," but I thought the London broker----.

MANUFACTURER: You see it's like this. Just as you associate a certain label with a particularly good brand of cigar so the planter's mark on the bag and the external appearance of the beans influence the broker by long association. But just as you cannot truly judge a cigar by the picture on the box, so the broker has to consider what is under the shell of the bean. One or two manufacturers go further, but don't trust merely to "tasting with their eyes"--they only come to a conclusion when they have roasted a sample.

PLANTER: But a buyer can get a shrewd idea without roasting, surely? You agree. Well, what exactly does he look for?

MANUFACTURER: Depends what nationality the bean is--I mean whether it was grown in Venezuela, Brazil, Trinidad, or the Gold Coast. In general he likes beans with a good "break," that is beans which, under the firm pressure of thumb and forefinger, break into small crisp nibs. Closeness or cheesiness are danger signals, warnings of lack of fermentation,--so is a slate-coloured interior. He prefers a pale, even-coloured interior,--cinnamon, chocolate, or café-au-lait colour and----.

PLANTER: One moment! I've heard before of planters being told to ferment and cure until the bean is cinnamon colour. Why, man, you couldn't get a pale brown interior with beans of the Forastero or Calabacillo type if you fermented them to rottenness.

MANUFACTURER: True! Well, if the breed on your plantation is purple Forastero, and more than half of the cacao in the world is, you must develop as much brown in the beans as possible. They should have the characteristic refreshing odour of raw cacao, together with a faint vinegary odour. The buyers much dislike any foreign smell, any mouldy, hammy, or cheesy odour.

PLANTER: And where do the foreign odours come from?

MANUFACTURER: That's debatable. Some come from bad fermentations, due to dirty fermentaries, abnormal temperatures, or unripe cacao.[7] Some come from smoky or imperfect artificial drying. Some come from mould. Unfermented cacao is liable to go mouldy, so is germinated or over-ripe cacao with broken shells. Some cacao unfortunately gets wet with sea water. There always seems to me something pathetic in the thought of finely-cured cacao being drowned in sea water as it goes out in open boats to the steamer.

PLANTER: You see, we haven't piers and jetties everywhere, and often it's a long journey to them. Well, you've told me the buyers note break, colour and aroma. Anything else?

MANUFACTURER: They like large beans, partly because largeness suggests fineness, and partly because with large beans the percentage of shell is less. Small flat beans are very wasteful and unsatisfactory; they are nearly all shell and very difficult to separate from the shell.

PLANTER: When there's a drought we can't help ourselves; we produce quantities of small flat beans.

MANUFACTURER: It must be trying to be at the mercy of the weather. However, the weather doesn't prevent the dirt being picked out of the beans. Buyers don't like more than half a per cent. of rubbish; I mean stones, dried twig-like pieces of pulp, dust, etc., left in the cacao, neither do they like to see "cobs," that is, two or more beans stuck together, nor----.

PLANTER: How about gloss?

MANUFACTURER: The beauty of a polished bean attracts, although they know the beauty is less than skin deep.

PLANTER: And washing?

MANUFACTURER: In my opinion washing is bad, leaves the shell too fragile. I believe in Hamburg they used to pay more for washed beans; although very little, I suppose less than five per cent., of the world's cacao is washed, but in London many buyers prefer "the great unwashed." However, brokers are conservative, and would probably look on unwashed Ceylon with suspicion.

PLANTER: Well, I have been very interested in everything that you have said, and I think every planter should strive to produce the very best he can, but he does not get much encouragement.

MANUFACTURER: How is that?

PLANTER: There is insufficient difference between the price of the best and the common.

MANUFACTURER: Unfortunately that is beyond any individual manufacturer's control. The price is controlled by the European and New York markets. I am afraid that as long as there is so large a demand by the public for cheap cocoas so long will there be keen competition amongst buyers for the commoner kinds of beans.

PLANTER: The manufacturer should keep some of his own men on the spot to do his buying. They would discriminate carefully, and the differences in price offered would soon educate the planters!

MANUFACTURER: True, but as each manufacturer requires cacao from many countries and districts, this would be a very costly enterprise. Several manufacturers have had their own buyers in certain places in the Tropics for some years, and it is generally agreed that this has acted as an incentive to the growers to improve the quality.[8] But in the main we have to look to the various Government Agricultural Departments to instruct and encourage the planters in the use of the best methods.

[7] Cameroon cacao sometimes has an objectionable odour and flavour, which may be due to its being fermented in an unripe condition, for, as Dr. Fickendey says: "Cameroon cacao has to be harvested unripe to save the pods from brown rot."

[8] The Director of Agriculture, in a paper on The Gold Coast Cocoa Industry, says: "We are indebted to Messrs. Cadbury Bros., of Bournville, for a lead in this direction. They have several agents in the colony who purchase on their behalf only the best

qualities at an enhanced price, and reject all that falls below the standard of their requirements."

[Illustration: THE WORLD'S CACAO PRODUCTION. (Mean of 5 years, 1914-1918. Average world production 295,600 tons per annum.) Diagram showing relative amounts produced by various countries. The shaded parts show production of British Possessions.]

CHAPTER IV

CACAO PRODUCTION AND SALE

When the English Commander, Thomas Candish, coming into the Haven Guatulco, burnt two hundred thousand tun of cacao, it proved no small loss to all New Spain, the provinces Guatimala and Nicaragua not producing so much in a whole year.

John Ogilvy's *America*, 1671.

When one starts to discuss, however briefly, the producing areas, one ought first to take off one's hat to Ecuador, for so long the principal producer, and then to Venezuela the land of the original cacao, and producer of the finest criollo type. Having done this, one ought to say words of praise to Trinidad, Grenada and Ceylon for their scientific methods of culture and preparation; and, last but not least, the newest and greatest producer, the Gold Coast, should receive honourable mention. It is interesting to note that in 1918 British Possessions produced nearly half (44 per cent.) of the world's supply.

Whilst the war has not very materially hindered the increase of cacao production in the tropics, the shortage of shipping has prevented the amount exported from maintaining a steady rise. The table below, taken mainly from the "Gordian," illustrates this:

WORLD PRODUCTION OF CACAO. Total in tons (1 ton = 1000 kilogrammes)

1908 194,000 1914 277,000 1909 206,000 1915 298,000 1910 220,000 1916 297,000 1911 241,000 1917 343,000 1912 234,000 1918 273,000 1913 258,000 1919 431,000

The following table is compiled chiefly from Messrs. Theo. Vasmer & Co.'s reports in the *Confectioners' Union*.

CACAO PRODUCTION OF THE CHIEF PRODUCING AREAS OF THE WORLD. (1 ton = 1000 kilogrammes).

Country. 1914 1915 1916 1917 1918 Tons. Tons. Tons. Tons. Tons. Gold Coast[1] 53,000 77,300 72,200 91,000 66,300 Brazil 40,800 45,000 43,700 55,600 41,900 Ecuador 47,200 37,000 42,700 47,200 38,000 San Thomé 31,400 29,900 33,200 31,900 26,600 Trinidad[1] 28,400 24,100 24,000 31,800 26,200 San Domingo 20,700 20,200 21,000 23,700 18,800 Venezuela 16,900 18,300 15,200 13,100 13,000 Lagos[1] 4,900 9,100 9,000 15,400 10,200 Grenada[1] 6,100 6,500 5,500 5,500 6,700 Fernando Po 3,100 3,900 3,800 3,700 4,200 Ceylon[1] 2,900 3,900 3,500 3,700 4,000 Jamaica[1] 3,800 3,600 3,400 2,800 3,000 Surinam 1,900 1,700 2,000 1,900 2,500 Cameroons 1,200 2,400 3,000 2,800 1,300 Haiti 2,100 1,800 1,900 1,500 2,300 French Cols. 1,800 1,900 1,600 2,200 1,700 Cuba 1,800 1,700 1,500 1,500 1,000 Java 1,600 1,500 1,500 1,600 800 Samoa 1,100 900 900 1,200 800 Togo 200 300 400 1,600 1,000 St. Lucia[1] 700 800 700 600 500 Belgian Congo 500 600 800 800 900 Dominica[1] 450 550 300 300 300 St. Vincent[1] 100 100 75 50 75 Other countries 3,200 3,000 3,500 3,500 3,500
--- Total 275,900 296,100 295,400 344,000 275,600 --- Total British Empire 102,000 128,000 120,000 153,000 119,000

[1] British Possessions.

[Illustration: MAP OF THE WORLD, WITH ONLY CACAO-PRODUCING AREAS MARKED.]

SOUTH AMERICAN CACAO.

In the map of South America given on p. 89 the principal cacao producing areas are marked. Their production in 1918 was as follows:

CACAO BEANS EXPORTED.

Percentage of Country. Metric Tons.[2] World's production.

Brazil 41,865 15.4 Ecuador 38,000 14.0 (Guayaquil alone 34,973 tons) Venezuela 13,000 5.0 Surinam 2,468 0.9 British Guiana 20 0.01 -- South American Total 95,353 tons 35.31 per cent. --

[2] These figures, and others quoted later in this chapter, are estimates given by Messrs. Theo. Vasmer & Co. in their reports.

ECUADOR.

Arriba and Machala Cacaos.--In Ecuador, for many years the chief producing area of the world, dwell the cacao kings, men who possess very large and wild cacao forests, each containing several million cacao trees. The method of culture is primitive, and no artificial manures are used, yet for several generations the trees have given good crops and the soil remains as fertile as ever. The two principal cacaos are known as *Arriba* and *Machala*, or classed together as Guayaquil after the city of that name. Guayaquil, the commercial metropolis of the Republic of Ecuador, is an ancient and picturesque city built almost astride the Equator. Despite the unscientific cultural methods, and the imperfect fermentation, which results in the cacao containing a high percentage of unfermented beans and not infrequently mouldy beans also, this cacao is much appreciated in Europe and America, for the beans are large and possess a fine strong flavour and characteristic scented aroma. The amount of Guayaquil cacao exported in 1919 was 33,209 tons.

[Illustration: RAKING CACAO BEANS ON THE DRIERS.]

[Illustration: GATHERING CACAO PODS IN ECUADOR. (La Clementina Plantation, Ecuador.)]

[Illustration: SORTING CACAO FOR SHIPMENT, GUAYAQUIL, ECUADOR.]

An interesting experiment was made in 1912, when a protective association known as the *Asociacion de Agricultores del Ecuador* was legalised. This collects half a golden dollar on every hundred pounds of cacao, and by purchasing and storing cacao on its own account whenever prices fall below a reasonable minimum, attempts in the planter's interest to regulate the selling price of cacao. Unfortunately, as cacao tends to go mouldy when stored in a damp tropical climate, the *Asociacion* is not an unmixed blessing to the manufacturer and consumer.

BRAZIL.

Parâ and Bahia Cacaos.--Brazil has made marked progress in recent years, and has now overtaken Ecuador in quantity of produce; the cacao, however, is quite different from, and not as fine as, that from Guayaquil. The principal cacao comes from the State of Bahia, where the climate is ideal for its cultivation. Indeed so perfect are the natural conditions that formerly no care was taken in cacao production, and much of that gathered was wild and uncured. During the last decade there has been an improvement, and this would, doubtless, be more noteworthy if the means of transport were better, for at present the roads are bad and the railways inadequate; hence most of the cacao is brought down to the city of Bahia in canoes. Nevertheless, Bahia cacao is better fermented than the peculiar cacao of Pará, another important cacao from Brazil, which is appreciated by manufacturers on account of its mild flavour. Bahia exported in 1919 about 51,000 tons of cacao.

VENEZUELA.

Caracas, Carupano and Maracaibo Cacaos.--Venezuela has been called "the classic home of cacao," and had not the chief occupation of its inhabitants been revolution, it would have retained till now the important position it held a hundred years ago. It is in this enchanted country (it was at La Guayra in Caracas, as readers of *Westward Ho!* will remember, that Amyas found his long-sought Rose) that the finest cacao in the world is produced: the criollo, the bean with the golden-brown break. The tree which produces this is as delicate as the cacao is fine, and there is some danger that this superb cacao may die out--a tragedy which every connoisseur would wish to avert.

The *Gordian* estimates that Venezuela sent out from her three principal ports in 1919 some 16,226 tons of cacao.

THE WEST INDIES.

In the map of South America the principal West Indian islands producing cacao are marked. Their production in 1918 was as follows:

CACAO BEANS EXPORTED. Percentage of Metric Tons. World's production. Trinidad (British) 26,177 9.7 San Domingo 18,839 7.0 Grenada (British) 6,704 2.5 Jamaica (British) 3,000 1.1 Haiti 2,272 0.8 St. Lucia (British) 500 0.2 Dominica (British) 300 0.1 St. Vincent (British) 70 0.02 ----------- --------------- West Indies Total 57,862 tons 21.42 per cent. ----------- --------------- Br. West Indies 36,751 tons 13.6 per cent.

TRINIDAD AND GRENADA.[3]

[3] Cacao production in 1919: Trinidad 27,185 tons; Grenada 4,020 tons.

Cacao was grown in the West Indies in the seventeenth century, and the inhabitants, after the destructive "blast," which utterly destroyed the plantations in 1727, bravely replanted cacao, which has flourished there ever since. The cacaos of Trinidad and Grenada have long been known for their excellence, and it is mainly from Trinidad that the knowledge of methods of scientific cultivation and preparation has been spread to planters all round the equator. The cacao from Trinidad (famous alike for its cacao and its pitch lake) has always held a high place in the markets of the world, although a year or two ago the inclusion of inferior cacao and the practice of claying was abused by a few growers and merchants. With the object of stopping these abuses and of producing a uniform cacao, there was formed a Cacao Planters' Association, whose business it is to grade and bulk, and sell on a co-operative basis, the cacao produced by its members. This experiment has proved successful, and in 1918 the Association handled the cacao from over 100 estates. We may expect to see more of these cacao planters' associations formed in various parts of the world, for they are in line with the trend of the times towards large, and ever larger, unions and combinations. Trinidad is also progressive in its system of agricultural education and in its formation of agricultural credit societies. The neighbouring island of Grenada is mountainous, smaller than the Isle of Wight and (if the Irish will forgive me) greener than Erin's Isle. The methods of cacao cultivation in vogue there might seem natural to the British farmer, but they are considered remarkable by cacao planters, for in Grenada the soil on which the trees grow is forked or tilled. Possibly from this follows the equally remarkable corollary that the cacao trees flourish without a single shade tree. The preparation of the bean receives as much care as the cultivation of the tree, and the cacao which comes from the estates has an unvaried constancy of quality, not infrequently giving 100 per cent. of perfectly prepared beans. It is largely due to this that the cacao from this small island occupies such an important position on the London market.

[Illustration: MAP OF SOUTH AMERICA AND THE WEST INDIES. Only cacao-producing areas are marked.]

[Illustration: WORKERS ON A CACAO PLANTATION. (Messrs. Cadbury's estate in Trinidad.)]

The cacao from San Domingo is known commercially as *Samana* or *Sanchez*. A fair proportion is of inferior quality, and is little appreciated on the European markets. The bulk of it goes to America. The production in 1919 was about 23,000 tons.

AFRICAN CACAO.

In the map of Africa the principal producing areas are marked. Their production in 1918 was as follows:

CACAO BEANS EXPORTED. Metric Tons. Percentage of World's production. Gold Coast (British) 66,343 24.5 San Thomé 19,185 7.1 Lagos (British) 10,223 3.8 Fernando Po 4,220 1.6 Cameroons 1,250 0.4 Togo 1,000 0.4 Belgian Congo 875 0.3 ------------ -------------- African Total 103,096 tons 38.1 per cent. ------------ -------------- British Africa 76,566 tons 28.3 per cent.

THE GOLD COAST (*Industria floremus*).

Accra Cacao.

The name recalls stories of a romantic and awful past, in which gold and the slave trade played their terrible part. Happily these are things of the past; so is the "deadly climate." We are told that it is now no worse than that of other tropical countries. According to Sir Hugh Clifford, until recently Governor of the Gold Coast, the "West African Climatic Bogie" is a myth, and the "monumental reputation for unhealthiness" undeserved. When De Candolle wrote concerning cacao, "I imagine it would succeed on the Guinea Coast,"[4] as the West African coast is sometimes called, he achieved prophecy, but he little dreamed how wonderful this success would be. The rise and growth of the cacao-growing industry in the Gold Coast is one of the most extraordinary developments of the last few decades. In thirty years it has increased its export of cacao from nothing to 40 per cent. of the total of the world's production.

[4] De Candolle, *Origin of Cultivated Plants*, quoted by R. Whymper.

[Illustration: MAP OF AFRICA--WITH ONLY CACAO-PRODUCING AREAS MARKED.]

[Illustration: FORESHORE AT ACCRA, WITH STACKS OF CACAO READY FOR SHIPMENT. Reproduced by permission of the Editor of "West Africa".]

PRODUCTION OF CACAO ON THE GOLD COAST.

Year. Quantity. Value. £ 1891 0 tons (80 lbs.) 4 1896 34 tons 2,276 1901 980 tons 42,837 1906 8,975 tons 336,269 1911 30,798 tons 1,613,468 1916 72,161 tons 3,847,720

1917 90,964 tons 3,146,851 1918 66,343 tons 1,796,985 1919 177,000 tons 8,000,000

The conditions of production in the Gold Coast present a number of features entirely novel. We hear from time to time of concessions being granted in tropical regions to this or that company of enterprising European capitalists, who employ a few Europeans and send them to the area to manage the industry. The inhabitants of the area become the manual wage earners of the company, and too often in the lust for profits, or as an offering to the god of commercial efficiency, the once easy and free life of the native is lost for ever and a form of wage-slavery takes its place with doubtful effects on the life and health of the workers. In defence it is pointed out that yet another portion of the earth has been made productive, which, without the initiative of the European capitalist, must have lain fallow. But in the Gold

Coast the "indolent" native has created a new industry entirely native owned, and in thirty years the Gold Coast has outstripped all the areas of the world in quantity of produce. Forty years ago the natives had never seen a cacao tree, now at least fifty million trees flourish in the colony. This could not have happened without the strenuous efforts of the Department of Agriculture. The Gold Coast now stands head and shoulders above any other producing area for quantity. The problem of the future lies in the improvement of quality, and difficult though this problem be, we cannot doubt, given a fair chance, that the far-sighted and energetic Agricultural Department will solve it. Indeed, it must in justice be pointed out that already a very marked improvement has been made, and now fifty to one hundred times as much good fermented cacao is produced as there was ten years ago.[5] However, if a high standard is to be maintained, the work of the Department of Agriculture must be supplemented by the willingness of the cacao buyers to pay a higher price for the better qualities.

[5] "Towards this latter result Messrs. Cadbury Bros., Ltd., rendered great assistance. This firm sent representatives into the country, who proved to the natives that they were willing to pay an enhanced price for cocoa prepared in a manner suitable for their requirements. A fair amount of cocoa was purchased by them, and demonstrations were made in some places with regard to the proper mode of fermentation." (The Agricultural and Forest Products of British West Africa. *Imperial Institute Handbook*, by G.C. Dudgeon).

[Illustration: CARRIERS CONVEYING BAGS OF CACAO TO SURF BOATS, ACCRA. Reproduced by permission of the Editor of "West Africa."]

The phenomenal growth of this industry is the more remarkable when we consider the lack of roads and beasts of burden. The usual pack animals, horses and oxen, cannot live on the Gold

Coast because of the tsetse fly, which spreads amongst them the sleeping sickness. And so the native, used as he is to heavy head-loads, naturally adopted this as his first method of transport, and hundreds of the less affluent natives arrive at the collecting centres with great weights of cacao on their heads. "Women and children, light-hearted, chattering and cheerful, bear their 60 lbs. head-loads with infinite patience. Heavier loads, approaching sometimes two hundredweight, are borne by grave, silent Hausa-men, often a distance of thirty or forty miles."

[Illustration: CROSSING THE RIVER AT NSAWAM, GOLD COAST.]

[Illustration: DRYING CACAO BEANS AT MRAMRA. Reproduced by permission from the Imperial Institute series of Handbooks to the Commercial Resources of the Tropics.]

One day, not so many years ago, some more ingenious native in the hills at the back of the Coast, filled an old palm-oil barrel with cacao and rolled it down the ways to Accra. And now to-day it is a familiar sight to see a man trundling a huge barrel of cacao, weighing half a ton, down to the coast. The sound of a motor horn is heard, and he wildly turns the barrel aside to avoid a disastrous collision with the new, weird transport animal from Europe. Motor lorries have been used with great effect on the coast for some seven years; they have the advantage over pack animals that they do not succumb to the bite of the dreaded tsetse fly, but nevertheless not a few derelicts lie, or stand on their heads, in the ditches, the victims of over-work or accident.

[Illustration: SHOOTING CACAO FROM THE ROAD TO THE BEACH, ACCRA.]

Having brought the cacao to the coast, there yet remains the lighterage to the ocean liner, which lies anchored some two miles from the shore, rising and falling to the great rollers from the broad Atlantic. A long boat is used, manned by some twenty swarthy natives, who glory--vocally--in their passage through the dangerous surf which roars along the sloping beach. The cacao is piled high on wood racks and covered with tarpaulins and seldom shares the fate of passengers and crew, who are often drenched in the surf before they swing by a crane in the primitive mammy chair, high but not dry, on board the hospitable Elder Dempster liner.

[Illustration: ROLLING CACAO, GOLD COAST.]

SAN THOMÉ (AND PRINCIPE).

We now turn from the Gold Coast and the success of native ownership to another part of West Africa, a scene of singular beauty, where the Portuguese planters have triumphed over savage nature.

Two lovely islands, San Thomé and its little sister isle of Principe, lie right on the Equator in the Gulf of Guinea, about two hundred miles from the African mainland. A warm, lazy sea, the sea of the doldrums, sapphire or turquoise, or, in deep shaded pools, a radiant green, joyfully foams itself away against these fairy lands of tossing palm, dense vegetation, rushing cascades, and purple, precipitous peaks. A soil of volcanic origin is covered with a rich humus of decaying vegetation, and this, with a soft humid atmosphere, makes an ideal home for cacao.

The bean, introduced in 1822, was not cultivated with diligence till fifty years ago. To-day the two islands, which together have not half the area of Surrey, grow 32,000 metric tons of cacao a year, or about one-tenth of the world's production.[6] The income of a single planter, once a poor peasant, has amounted to hundreds of thousands sterling.

[6] The *Gordian's* estimate for the amount exported in 1919 is 40,766 tons.

[Illustration: ROLLING CACAO, GOLD COAST. Reproduced by permission of the Editor of "West Africa."]

Dotted over the islands, here nestling on a mountain side, there overlooking some blue inlet of the sea, are more than two hundred plantations, or *rocas*, whose buildings look like islands in a green sea of cacao shrubs, above which rise the grey stems of such forest trees as have been left to afford shade.

[Illustration: CARRYING CACAO TO THE RAILWAY STATION, NSAWAM, GOLD COAST.]

Here, not only have the cultivation, fermentation and drying of cacao been brought to the highest state of perfection, but the details of organisation--planters' homes, hospitals, cottages, drying sheds and the Decauville railways--are often models of their kind.

Intelligent and courteous, the planters make delightful hosts. At their homes, five thousand miles away from Europe, the visitor, who knows what it means to struggle with steaming, virgin forests, rank encroaching vegetation, deadly fevers, and the physical and mental inertia engendered by the tropics, will marvel at the courage and energy that have triumphed over such obstacles. Calculating from various estimates, each labourer in the islands appears to produce about 1,640 pounds of cacao yearly, and the average yield per cultivated acre is 480 pounds, or about 30 pounds more than that of Trinidad in 1898.

[Illustration: WAGON LOADS OF CACAO BEING TAKEN FROM MESSRS. CADBURY'S DEPOT TO THE BEACH, ACCRA.]

As there is no available labour in San Thomé, the planters get their workers from the mainland of Africa. Prior to the year 1908, the labour system of the islands was responsible for grave abuses. This has now been changed. Natives from the Portuguese colonies of Angola and Mozambique now enter freely into contracts ranging from one to five years, two years being the time generally chosen. At the end of their term of work they either re-contract or return to their native land with their savings, with which they generally buy a wife. The readiness with which the natives volunteer for the work on the islands is proof both of the soundness of the system of contract and of the good treatment they receive at the hands of the planters.

[Illustration: THE BUILDINGS OF THE BOA ENTRADA CACAO ESTATE, SAN THOMÉ.]

Unfortunately, the mortality of the plantation labourers has generally been very heavy, one large and well-managed estate recording on an average of seven years an annual death rate of 148 per thousand, and many *rocas* have still more appalling records. Against this, other plantations only a few miles away may show a mortality approximating to that of an average European city. In February, 1918, the workers in San Thomé numbered 39,605, and the deaths during the previous year, 1917, were 1,808, thus showing on official figures an annual mortality of 45 per thousand. Comparing this with the 26 per thousand of Trinidad, and remembering that most of the San Thomé labourers are in the prime of life, it will be seen that this death rate represents a heavy loss of life and justifies the continued demand from the British cocoa manufacturers for the appointment and report of a special medical commission.

The Portuguese Government is prepared to meet this demand, for it has recently sent a Commissioner, Dr. Joaquim Gouveia, to San Thomé to make a thorough examination of labour conditions, including work, food, housing, hospitals and medical attendance, and to report fully and confidentially to the Portuguese Colonial Secretary.

[Illustration: DRYING CACAO AT AGUA IZE, SAN THOMÉ. The trays are on wheels, which run on rails.]

If this important step is followed by adequate measures of reform there is every reason to hope that the result will be a material reduction in the death rate, as the good health enjoyed on some of the *rocas* shows San Thomé to be not more unhealthy than other tropical islands.

CAMEROONS.

The Cameroons, which we took from the Germans in 1916, is also on the West Coast of Africa. It lags far behind the Gold Coast in output, although both commenced to grow cacao about the same time. The Germans spent great sums in the Cameroons in giving the industry a scientific basis, they adopted the "estate plan," and possibly the fact that they employ contract labour explains why they have not had the same phenomenal success that the natives working for themselves have achieved on the Gold Coast.

[Illustration: BARREL ROLLING, GOLD COAST.]

Various countries and districts which are responsible for about 97 per cent. of the world's cacao crop have now been named and briefly commented upon. Of other producing areas, the islands, Ceylon and Java, are worthy of mention. In both of these (as also in Venezuela, Samoa[7] and Madagascar) is grown the criollo cacao, which produces the plump, sweet beans with the cinnamon "break." Cacao beans from Ceylon or Java are easily recognised by their appearance, because, being washed, they have beautiful clean shells, but there is a serious objection to washed shells, namely, that they are brittle and as thin as paper, so that many are broken before they reach the manufacturer. Ceylon is justly famous for its fine "old red"; along with this a fair quantity of inferior cacao is produced, which by being called Ceylon (such is the power of a good name), tends to claim a higher price than its quality warrants.

[7] Robert Louis Stevenson was one of the pioneers in cacao planting in Samoa, as readers of his *Vailima Letters* will remember.

[Illustration: BAGGING CACAO, GOLD COAST. Reproduced by permission of the Editor of "West Africa."]

CACAO MARKETS.

From the Plantation to the European Market.

It is mentioned above that on the Gold Coast cacao is brought down to Accra as head-loads, or in barrels, or in motor-lorries. These methods are exceptional; in other countries it is usually put in sacks at the estate. Every estate has its own characteristic mark, which is stamped on the bags, and this is recognised by the buyers in Europe, and gives a clue to the quality of the contents. There is not as yet a uniform weight for a bag of cacao, although they all vary between one and two cwt., thus the bags from Africa contain 1-1/4 cwts., whilst those from Guayaquil contain 1-3/4 cwts. In these bags the cacao is taken to the port on the backs of mules, in horse or ox carts, in canoes down a stream, or more rarely, by rail. It is then conveyed by lighters or surf boats to the great ocean liners which lie anchored off the shore. In the hold of the liner it is rocked thousands of miles over the azure seas of the tropics to the grey-green seas of the temperate zone. In pre-war days a million bags used to go to Hamburg, three-quarters of a million to New York, half a million to Havre, and only a trifling quarter of a million to London. Now London is the leading cacao market of the world. During the war the supplies were cut off from Hamburg, whilst Liverpool, becoming a chief port for African cacao, in 1916 imported a million bags. Then New York began to gorge cacao, and in 1917 created a record, importing some two and a half million bags, or about 150,000 tons. Whilst everything is in so fluid a condition it is unwise to prophesy; it may, however, be said that there are many who think, now that the consumption of cocoa and chocolate in America has reached such a prodigious figure, that New York may yet oust London and become the central dominating market of the world.

[Illustration: SURF BOATS BY THE SIDE OF THE OCEAN LINER, ACCRA.]

Difficulties of Buying.

Every country produces a different kind of cacao, and the cacao from any two plantations in the same country often shows wide variation. It may be said that there are as many kinds of cacao as there are of apples, cacao showing as marked differences as exhibited by crabs and Blenheims, not to mention James Grieves, Russets, Worcester Pearmains, Newton Wonders, Lord Derbys, Belle de Boskoops, and so forth. Further, whilst the bulk of the cacao is good and sound, a little of the cacao grown in any district is liable to have suffered from drought or from attacks by moulds or insect pests. It will be realised from these fragmentary remarks that the buyer must exercise perpetual vigilance.

[Illustration: BAGGING CACAO BEANS FOR SHIPMENT, TRINIDAD.]

[Illustration: TRANSFERRING BAGS OF CACAO BEANS TO LIGHTERS, TRINIDAD.]

Cacao Sales.

Before the Cocoa Prices Orders were published (March, 1918) the manner of conducting the sale of cacao in London was as follows. Brokers' lists giving the kinds of cacao for sale, and the number of bags of each, were sent, together with samples, to the buyers some days beforehand, so that they were able to decide what they wished to purchase and the price they were willing to pay. The sales always took place at 11 o'clock on Tuesdays in the Commercial Sale Room in Mincing Lane, that narrow street off Fenchurch Street, where the air is so highly charged with expert knowledge of the world's produce, that it would illuminate the prosaic surroundings with brilliant flashes if it could become visible. On the morning of the sale samples of the cacaos are on exhibit at the principal brokers. The man in the street brought into the broker's office would ask what these strange beans might be. "A new kind of almond?" he might ask. And then, on being told they were cacao, he would see nothing to choose between all the various lots and wonder why so much fuss was made over discriminating amongst the similar and distinguishing the identical. He might even marvel a little at the expert knowledge of the buyers; yet, frankly, the pertinent facts concerning quality, known by the buyer, are fewer and no more difficult to learn than the thousand and one facts a lad must have at his finger ends to pass the London Matriculation; they are valued because they are inaccessible to the multitude; only a few people have the opportunity of learning them, and their use may make or mar fortunes. The judgment of quality is, however, only one side of the art of buying. We have to add to these a knowledge of the conditions prevailing in the various markets of the world, a knowledge of stocks and probable supplies, and given this knowledge, an ability to estimate their effect, together with other conditions, agricultural, political and social, on the price of the commodity. The room in which the sales are conducted is not a large one, and usually not more than a hundred people, buyers, pressmen, etc., are present. Not a single cacao bean is visible, and it might be an auction sale of property for all the uninitiated could tell. The cacao is put up in lots. Usually the sales proceed quietly, and it is difficult to realize that many thousands of bags of cacao are changing hands. The buyers have perfect trust in the broker's descriptions; they know the invariable fair-play of the British broker, which is a by-word the world over. The machinery of the proceedings is lubricated by an easy flow of humour. Sometimes a few bags of sea-damaged cacao or of cacao sweepings are put up, and a good deal of keenness is shown by the individuals who buy this stuff. It is curious that a whole crowd of busy people will allow their time to be taken up whilst there is a spirited fight between two or three buyers for a single bag.

Whilst the London Auction Sales are of importance as fixing the prices for the various markets, and reflecting to a certain extent the position of supply and demand, only a fraction of the world's cacao changes hands at the Auction Sales, the greater part of it being bought privately for forward delivery.

Prices and Quotations.

[Illustration: DIAGRAM SHOWING VARIATION IN PRICE OF CACAO BEANS FROM 1913 TO 1919.]

The price of cacao is liable to fluctuations like every other product, thus in 1907 Trinidad cacao rose to one shilling a pound, whilst there have been periods when it has only fetched sixpence per pound. On April 2nd, 1918, the Food Controller fixed the prices of the finest qualities of the different varieties of raw cacao as follows:

British West Africa (Accra) 65s. per cwt.

Bahia } Cameroons } San Thomé } 85s. " " Congo } Grenada }

Trinidad } Demerara } 90s. " " Guayaquil } Surinam }

Ceylon } Java } 100s. " " Samoa }

The diagram on p. 113 shows the average market price in the United Kingdom of some of the more important cacaos before, during, and after the war. The most striking change is the sudden rise when the Government control was removed. All cacaos showed a substantial advance varying from 80 to 150 per cent. on pre-war values. Further large advances have taken place in the early months of 1920.

The Call of the Tropics.

Many a young man, reading in some delightful book of travel, has longed to go to the tropics and see the wonders for himself. There can be no doubt that a sojourn in equatorial regions is one of the most educative of experiences. In support of this I cannot do better than quote Grant Allen, who regarded the tropics as the best of all universities. "But above all in educational importance I rank the advantage of seeing human nature in its primitive surroundings, far from the squalid and chilly influences of the tail-end of the Glacial epoch." ... "We must forget all this formal modern life; we must break away from this cramped, cold, northern world; we must find ourselves face to face at last, in Pacific isles or African forests, with the underlying truths of simple naked nature."

[Illustration: GROUP OF WORKERS ON CACAO ESTATE.

Some are standing on the Drying Platform, which is the roof of the Fermentary.]

Many will recall how Charles Kingsley's longing to see the tropics was ultimately satisfied. In his book, in which he describes how he "At Last" visited the West Indies, we read that he encountered a happy Scotchman living a quiet life in the dear little island of Monos. "I looked at the natural beauty and repose; at the human vigour and happiness; and I said to myself, and said it often afterwards in the West Indies: 'Why do not other people copy this wise Scot? Why should not many a young couple, who have education, refinement, resources in themselves, but are, happily or unhappily for them, unable to keep a brougham and go to London balls, retreat to some such paradise as this (and there are hundreds like it to be found in the West Indies), leaving behind them false civilisation, and vain desires, and useless show; and there live in simplicity and content 'The Gentle Life'?"

The Planter's Life.

Few who go to the tropics escape their fascination, and of those that are young, few return to colder climes. Some become overseers, others, more fortunate, own the estates they manage. It is inadvisable for the inexperienced to start on the enterprise of buying and planting an estate with less capital than two or three thousand pounds; but, once established, a cacao plantation may be looked upon as a permanent investment, which will continue to bear and give a good yield as long as it receives proper attention.

In the recently published *Letters of Anthony Farley* the writer tells how Farley encounters in South America an old college friend of his, who in his early days was on the high road to a brilliant political career. Here he is, a planter. He explains:

"My mother was Spanish; her brother owned this place. When he died it came to me."

"How did your uncle hold it through the various revolutions?"

"Nothing simpler. He became an American citizen. When trouble threatened he made a bee-line for the United States Consulate. I'm British, of course. Well, just when I had decided upon a political life, I found it necessary to come here to straighten things out. One month lengthened itself into a year. I grew fascinated. Here I felt a sense of immense usefulness. On the mountain side my coffee-trees flourished; down in the valley grew cacao."

"I grow mine on undulations."

"You needn't, you know, so long as you drain."

"Yes, but draining on the flat is the devil."

"Anyhow, I always liked animals--you haven't seen my pigs yet--and horses and mules need careful tending. A cable arrived one morning announcing an impending dissolution. I felt like an unwilling bridegroom called to marry an ugly bride. I invited my soul. Here, thought I to myself, are animals and foodstuffs--good, honest food at that. If I go back it is only to fill people's bellies with political east wind.

"To come to the point, I decided to grow coffee and cacao. I cabled infinite regrets. The decision once made, I was happy as a sandboy. *J'y suis, j'y reste*, said I to myself, said I. Nor have I ever cast one longing look behind."[8]

[8] Quoted from the *New Age*, where the *Letters of Anthony Farley* first appeared.

This is fiction, but I think it is true that very few, if any, who become planters in the tropics ever return permanently to England. The hospitality of the planters is proverbial: there must be something good and free about the planter's life to produce men so genial and generous. There is a picture that I often recall, and never without pleasure. A young planter and I had, with the help of more or less willing mules, climbed over the hills from one valley to the next. The valley we had left is noted for its beauty, but to me it had become familiar; the other valley I saw now for the first time. The sides were steep and covered with trees, and I could only see one dwelling in the valley. We reached this by a circuitous path through cacao trees. Approaching it as we did, the bungalow seemed completely cut off from the rest of the world. We were welcomed by the planter and his wife, and by those of the children who were not shy. I have never seen more chubby or jolly kiddies, and I know from the sweetness of the children that their mother must have given them unremitting attention. I wondered indeed if she ever left them for a moment. I knew, too, from the situation of the bungalow in the heart of the hills that visitors were not likely to be frequent. The planter's life is splendid for a man who likes open air and nature, but I had sometimes thought that their wives would not find the life so good. I was mistaken. When we came away, after riding some distance, through a gap in the cacao we saw across the valley a group of happy children. They saw us, and all of them, even the shy ones, waved us adieux.

[Illustration: CARTING CACAO TO RAILWAY STATION, CEYLON.]

[Illustration: THE CARENAGE, GRENADA.]

CHAPTER V

THE MANUFACTURE OF COCOA AND CHOCOLATE

The Indians, from whom we borrow it, are not very nice in doing it; they roast the kernels in earthen pots, then free them from their skins, and afterwards crush and grind them between two stones, and so form cakes of it with their hands.

Natural History of Chocolate, R. Brookes, 1730.

Early Methods in the Tropics.

As the cacao bean is grown in tropical countries, it is there that we must look for the first attempts at manufacturing from it a drink or a foodstuff. The primitive method of preparation was very simple, consisting in roasting the beans in a pot or on a shovel to develop their flavour, winnowing in the wind, and then rubbing the broken shelled beans between stones until quite fine. The curious thing is that on grinding the cacao bean in the heat of a tropical day we do not produce a powder but a paste. This is because half the cacao bean consists of a fat which is liquid at 90° F., a temperature which is reached in the shade in tropical countries. This paste was then made into small rolls and put in a cool place to set. Thus was produced the primitive unsweetened drinking chocolate. This is the method, which Elizabethans, who ventured into the tangled forests of equatorial America, found in use; and this is the method they brought home to Europe. In the tropics these simple processes are followed to this day, but in Europe they have undergone many elaborations and refinements.

If the reader will look at the illustration entitled "Women grinding chocolate," he will see how the brittle roasted bean is reduced to a paste in primitive manufacture. A stone, shaped like a rolling-pin, is being pushed to and fro over a concave slab, on which the smashed beans have already been reduced to a paste of a doughy consistency.

[Illustration: EARLY FACTORY METHODS. Fig. 1 is a workman roasting the cacao in an iron kettle over a furnace. He has to stir the beans to keep them from burning. Fig. 2 is a person sifting and freeing the roasted kernels (which when broken into fragments are called "*nibs*") from their husks or shell. Fig. 3 shows a workman pounding the shell-free nibs in an iron mortar. Fig. 4 represents a workman grinding the nibs on a hard smooth stone with an iron roller. The grinding is performed over a chafing-dish of burning charcoal, as it is necessary, for ease of grinding, to keep the paste in a liquid condition.]

Early European Manufacture.

The conversion of these small scale operations into the early factory process is well shown in the plate which I reproduce above from *Arts and Sciences*, published in 1768.

[Illustration: WOMEN GRINDING CHOCOLATE. From Squier "Nicaragua"]

A certain atmosphere of dreamy intellectuality is associated with coffee, so that the roasting of it is felt to be a romantic occupation. The same poetic atmosphere surrounded the manufacture of drinking chocolate in the early days: the writers who revealed the secrets of its preparation were conscious that they were giving man a new æsthetic delight and the subject is treated lovingly and lingeringly. One, Pietro Metastasio, went so far as to write a "cantata" describing its manufacture. He describes the grinding as being done by a vigorous man, and truly, to grind by hand is a very laborious operation, which happily in more recent times has been performed by the use of power-driven mills.

Operations on a large scale followed the founding of Fry and Sons at Bristol in 1728, and of Lombart, "la plus ancienne chocolaterie de France," in Paris in 1760. In Germany the first chocolate factory was erected at Steinhunde in 1756, under the patronage of Prince Wilhelm, whilst in America the well-known firm of Walter Baker and Co. began in a small way in 1765. From the methods adopted in these factories have gradually developed the modern processes which I am about to describe.

MODERN PRACTICE.

As the early stages in the manufacture of cocoa and of chocolate are often identical, the processes which are common to both are first described, and then some individual consideration is given to each.

(*a*) *Arrival at the Factory.*

The cacao is largely stored in warehouses, from which it is removed as required. It has remarkable keeping properties, and can be kept in a good store for several years without loss of quality. Samples of cacao beans in glass bottles have been found to be in perfect condition after thirty years. Some factories have stores in which stand thousands of bags of cacao drawn from many ports round the equator. There is something very pleasing about huge stacks of bags of cacao seen against the luminous white walls of a well-lighted store. The symmetry of their construction, and the continued repetition of the same form, are never better shown than when the men, climbing up the sides of a stack against which they look small, unbuild the mighty heap, the bags falling on to a continuous band which carries them jauntily out of the store.

[Illustration: PART OF A CACAO BEAN WAREHOUSE, SHOWING ENDLESS BAND CONVEYOR. (Messrs. Cadbury Bros'. Works, Bournville).]

(*b*) *Sorting the Beans.*

As all cacao is liable to contain a little free shell, dried pulp (often taken for twigs), threads of sacking and other foreign matter, it is very carefully sieved and sorted before passing on to the roasting shop. In this process curios are occasionally separated, such as palm kernels, cowrie shells, shea butter nuts, good luck seeds and "crab's eyes." The essential part of one type of machine (*see illustration*) which accomplishes this sorting is an inclined revolving cylinder of wire gauze along which the beans pass. The cylinder forms a continuous set of sieves of different sized mesh, one sieve allowing only sand to pass, another only very small beans or fragments of beans, and finally one holding back anything larger than single beans (*e.g.*, "cobs," that is, a collection of two or more beans stuck together).

[Illustration: CACAO BEAN SORTING AND CLEANING MACHINE. Reproduced by permission of Messrs. J. Baker & Sons, Ltd., Willesden.]

Another type of cleaning machine is illustrated by the diagram on the opposite page.

This machine with its shaking sieves and blast of air makes a great clatter and fuss. It produces, however, what the manufacturers desire--a clean bean sorted to size.

[Illustration: DIAGRAM OF CACAO BEAN CLEANING MACHINE. This is a box fitted with shaking sieves down which the cacao beans pass in a current of air. Having come over some large and very powerful magnets, which take out any nails or fragments of iron, they fall on to a sieve (1/4-inch holes) which the engineer describes as "rapidly reciprocating and arranged on a slight incline and mounted on spring bars." This allows grit to pass through. The beans then roll down a plane on to a sieve (3/8-inch holes) which separates the broken beans, and finally on to a sieve with oblong holes which allows the beans to fall through whilst retaining the clusters. The beans encounter a strong blast of air which brushes from them any shell or dust clinging to them.]

(c) *Roasting the Beans.*

As with coffee so with cacao, the characteristic flavour and aroma are only developed on roasting. Messrs. Bainbridge and Davies (chemists to Messrs. Rowntree) have shown that the aroma of cacao is chiefly due to an amazingly minute quantity (0.0006 per cent.) of linalool, a colourless liquid with a powerful fragrant odour, a modification of which occurs in bergamot, coriander and lavender. Everyone notices the aromatic odour which permeates the atmosphere round a chocolate factory. This odour is a bye-product of the roasting shop; possibly some day an enterprising chemist will prevent its escape or capture it, and sell it in bottles for flavouring confectionery, but for the present it serves only to announce in an appetising way the presence of a cocoa or chocolate works.

[Illustration: SECTION THROUGH GAS HEATED CACAO ROASTER.]

Roasting is a delicate operation requiring experience and discretion. Even in these days of scientific management it remains as much an art as a science. It is conducted in revolving drums to ensure constant agitation, the drums being heated either over coke fires or by gas. Less frequently the heating is effected by a hot blast of air or by having inside the drum a number of pipes containing super-heated steam.

[Illustration: ROASTING CACAO BEANS. (Messrs. Cadbury Bros'. Works, Bournville).]

The diagram and photo show one of the types of roasting machines used at Bournville. It resembles an ordinary coffee roaster, the beans being fed in through a hopper and heated by gas in the slowly revolving cylinder. The beans can be heard lightly tumbling one over the other, and the aroma round the roaster increases in fullness as they get hotter and hotter. The temperature which the beans reach in ordinary roasting is not very high, varying round 135° C. (275° F), and the average period of roasting is about one hour. The amount of loss of weight on roasting is considerable (some seven or eight per cent.), and varies with the amount of moisture present in the raw beans.

There have been attempts to replace the æsthetic judgment of man, as to the point at which to stop roasting, by scientific machinery. One rather interesting machine was so devised that the cacao roasting drum was fitted with a sort of steelyard, and this, when the loss of weight due to roasting had reached a certain amount, swung over and rang a bell, indicating dramatically that the roasting was finished. As beans vary amongst other things in the percentage of moisture which they contain, the machine has not replaced the experienced operator. He takes samples from the drum from time to time, and when the aroma has the character desired, the beans are rapidly discharged into a trolley with a perforated bottom, which is brought over a cold current of air. The object of this refinement is to stop the roasting instantly and prevent even a suspicion of burning.

After roasting, the shell is brittle and quite free from the cotyledons or kernel. The kernel has become glossy and friable and chocolate brown in colour, and it crushes readily between the fingers into small angular fragments (the "nibs" of commerce), giving off during the breaking down a rich warm odour of chocolate.

(d) *Removing the Shells.*

It has been stated (see *Fatty Foods*, by Revis and Bolton) that it was formerly the practice not to remove the shell. This is incorrect, the more usual practice from the earliest times has been to remove the shells, though not so completely as they are removed by the efficient machinery of to-day.

[Illustration: CACAO BEAN, SHELL AND GERM.]

In *A Curious Treatise on the Nature and Quality of Chocolate*, by Antonio Colmenero de Ledesma (1685), we read: "And if you peel the cacao, and take it out of its little shell, the drink thereof will be more dainty and delicious." Willoughby, in his *Travels in Spain*, (1664), writes: "They first toast the berries to get off the husk," and R. Brookes, in the *Natural History of Chocolate* (1730), says: "The Indians ... roast the kernels in earthen pots, then free them from their skins, and afterwards crush and grind them between two stones."

He further definitely recommends that the beans "be roasted enough to have their skins come off easily, which should be done one by one, laying them apart ... for these skins being left among the chocolate, will not dissolve in any liquor, nor even in the stomach, and fall to the bottom of the chocolate-cups as if the kernels had not been cleaned."

That the "Indian" practice of removing the shells was followed from the commencement of the industry in England, is shown by the old plate which we have reproduced on p. 120 from *Arts and Sciences*.

The removal of the shell, which in the raw condition is tough and adheres to the kernel, is greatly facilitated by roasting. If we place a roasted bean in the palm of the hand and press it with the thumb, the whole cracks up into crisp pieces. It is now quite easy to blow away the thin pieces of shell because they offer a greater surface to the air and are lighter than the compact little lumps or "nibs" which are left behind. This illustrates the principle of all shelling or husking machines.

(*e*) *Breaking the Bean into Fragments.*

The problem is to break down the bean to just the right size. The pieces must be sufficiently small to allow the nib and shell readily to part company, but it is important to remember that the smaller the pieces of shell and nib, the less efficient will the winnowing be, and it is usual to break the beans whilst they are still warm to avoid producing particles of extreme fineness. The breaking down may be accomplished by passing the beans through a pair of rollers at such a distance apart that the bean is cracked without being crushed. Or it may be effected in other ways, *e.g.*, by the use of an adjustable serrated cone revolving in a serrated conical case. In the diagram they are called kibbling cones.

[Illustration: SECTION THROUGH KIBBLING CONES AND GERM SCREENS.]

(*f*) *Separating the Germs.*

About one per cent. of the cacao bean fragments consists of "germs." The "germ" is the radicle of the cacao seed, or that part of the cacao seed which on germination forms the root. The germs are small and rod-shaped, and being very hard are generally assumed to be less digestible than the nib. They are separated by being passed through revolving gauze drums, the holes in which are the same size and shape as the germs, so that the germs pass through whilst the nib is retained. If a freakish carpenter were to try separating shop-floor sweepings, consisting of a jumble of chunks of wood (nib), shavings (shell) and nails (germ) by sieving through a grid-iron, he would find that not only the nails passed through but also some sawdust and fine shavings. So in the above machine the finer nib and shell pass through with the germ. This germ mixture, known as "smalls" is dealt with in a special machine, whilst the larger nib and shell are conveyed to the chief winnowing machine. In this machine the mixture is first sorted according to size and then the nib and shell separated from one another. The mixture is passed down long revolving cylindrical sieves and encounters a larger and larger mesh as it proceeds, and thus becomes sieved into various sizes. The separation of the shell from the nib is now effected by a powerful current of air, the large nib falling against the current, whilst the shell is carried with it and drops into another compartment. It is amusing to stand and watch the continuous stream of nibs rushing down, like hail in a storm, into the screw conveyor.

[Illustration: SECTION THROUGH WINNOWING MACHINE.]

This is the process in essence--to follow the various partially separated mixtures of shell and nib through the several further separating machines would be tedious; it is sufficient for the reader to know that after the most elaborate precautions have been taken the nib still contains about one per cent. of shell, and that the nib obtained is only 78.5 per cent. of the weight of raw beans originally taken. Most of the larger makers of cocoa produce nib containing less than two per cent. of shell, a standard which can only be maintained by continuous vigilance.

[Illustration: CACAO GRINDING. A battery of horizontal grinding mills, by which the cacao nibs are ground to paste (Messrs. Cadbury Bros., Bournville.)]

The shell, the only waste material of any importance produced in a chocolate factory, goes straight into sacks ready for sale. The pure cacao nibs (once an important article of commerce) proceed to the blenders and thence to the grinding mill.

(g) Blending.

We have seen that the beans are roasted separately according to their kind and country so as to develop in each its characteristic flavour. The pure nib is now blended in proportions which are carefully chosen to attain the result desired.

(h) Grinding the Cacao Nibs to Produce Mass.

In this process, by the mere act of grinding, the miracle is performed of converting the brittle fragments of the cacao bean into a chocolate-coloured fluid. Half of the cacao bean is fat, and the grinding breaks up the cells and liberates the fat, which at blood heat melts to an oil. Any of the various machines used in the industries for grinding might be used, but a special type of mill has been devised for the purpose.

In the grinding room of a cocoa factory one becomes almost hypnotised by a hundred of these circular mill-stones that rotate incessantly day and night. In Messrs. Fry's factory the "giddy motion of the whirling mill" is very much increased by a number of magnificent horizontal driving wheels, each some 20 feet in diameter, which form, as it were, a revolving ceiling to the room. Your fascinated gaze beholds "two or three vast circles, that have their revolving satellites like moons, each on its own axis, and each governed by master wheels. Watch them for any length of time and you might find yourself presently going round and round with them until you whirled yourself out of existence, like the gyrating maiden in the fairy tale."

In this type of grinding machine one mill stone rotates on a fixed stone. The cacao nib falls from a hopper through a hole in the centre of the upper stone and, owing to the manner in which grooves are cut in the two surfaces in contact, is gradually dragged between the stones. The grooves are so cut in the two stones that they point in opposite directions, and as the one stone revolves on the other, a slicing or shearing action is produced. The friction, due to the slicing and shearing of the nib, keeps the stones hot, and they become sufficiently warm to melt the fat in the ground nib, so that there oozes from the outer edge of the bottom or fixed stone a more or less viscous liquid or paste. This finely ground nib is known as "mass." It is simply liquified cacao bean, and solidifies on cooling to a chocolate coloured block.

[Illustration: SECTION THROUGH GRINDING STONES.]

This "mass" may be used for the production of either cocoa or chocolate. When part of the fat (cacao butter) is *taken away* the residue may be made to yield cocoa. When sugar and cacao butter are *added* it yields eating chocolate. Thus the two industries are seen to be inter-dependent, the cacao butter which is pressed out of the mass in the manufacture of cocoa being used up in the production of chocolate. The manufacture of cocoa will first be considered.

(*i*) *Pressing out the excess of Butter.*

The liquified cacao bean or "mass," simply mixed with sugar and cooled until it becomes a hard cake, has been used by the British Navy for a hundred years or more for the preparation of Jack's cup of cocoa. It produces a fine rich drink much appreciated by our hardy seamen, but it is somewhat too fatty to mix evenly with water, and too rich to be suitable for those with delicate digestions. Hence for the ordinary cocoa of commerce it is usual to remove a portion of this fat.

[Illustration: A CACAO PRESS. Reproduced by permission of Messrs. Lake, Orr & Co., Ltd.]

If "mass" be put into a cloth and pressed, a golden oil (melted cacao butter) oozes through the cloth. In practice this extraction of the butter is done in various types of presses. In one of the most frequently used types, the mass is poured into circular steel pots, the top and bottom of which are loose perforated plates lined with felt pads. A number of such pots are placed one above another, and then rammed together by a powerful hydraulic ram. They look like the parts of a slowly collapsing telescope. The "mass" is only gently pressed at first, but as the butter flows away and the material in the pot becomes stiffer, it is subjected to a gradually increasing pressure. The ram, being under pressure supplied by pumps, pushes up with enormous force. The steel pots have to be sufficiently strong to bear a great strain, as the ram often exerts a pressure of 6,000 pounds per square inch. When the required amount of butter has been pressed out, the pot is found to contain not a paste, but a hard dry cake of compressed cocoa. The liquified cacao bean put into the pots contains 54 to 55 per cent. of butter, whilst the cocoa press-cake taken out usually contains only 25 to 30 per cent. The expressed butter flows away and is filtered and solidified (see page 158). All that it is necessary to do to obtain cocoa from the press cake is to powder it.

[Illustration: SECTION THROUGH CACAO PRESS-POT AND RAM-PLATE.]

(j) Breaking Down the Press Cake to Cocoa Powder.

The slabs of press-cake are so hard and tough that if one were banged on a man's head it would probably stun him. They are broken down in a crushing mill, the inside of which is as full of terrible teeth as a giant's mouth, until the fragments are small enough to grind on steel rollers.

(k) Sieving.

As fineness is a very important quality of cocoa, the powder so obtained is very carefully sieved. This is effected by shaking the powder into an inclined rotating drum which is covered with silk gauze. In the cocoa which passes through this fine silk sieve, the average length of the individual particles is about 0.001 inch, whilst in first-class productions the size of the larger particles in the cocoa does not average more than 0.002 inch. Indeed, the cocoa powder is so fine that in spite of all precautions a certain amount always floats about in the air of sieving rooms, and covers everything with a brown film.

(l) Packing.

The cocoa powder is taken to the packing rooms. Here the tedious weighing by hand has been replaced by ingenious machines, which deliver with remarkable accuracy a definite weight of cocoa into the paper bag which lines the tin. The tins are then labelled and packed in cases ready for the grocer.

CHAPTER VI

THE MANUFACTURE OF CHOCOLATE

Since the great improvements of the steam engine, it is astonishing to what a variety of manufactures this useful machine has been applied: yet it does not a little excite our surprise that one is used for the trifling object of grinding chocolate.

It is, however, a fact, or at least, we are credibly informed, that Mr. Fry, of Bristol, has in his new manufactory one of these engines for the sole purpose of manufacturing chocolate and cocoa.

Berrow's Worcester Journal, June 7th, 1798.

What I am about to write under this heading will only be of a general character. Those who require a more detailed exposition are referred to the standard works given at the end of the chapter. In these, full and accurate information will be found. The information published in modern Encyclopædias, etc., concerning the manufacture of chocolate is not always as reliable as one might expect. Thus it states in Jack's excellent *Reference Book* (1914) that "Chocolate is made by the addition of water and sugar." The use of water in the manufacture of chocolate is contrary to all usual practice, so much so that great interest was aroused in the trade some years ago by the statement that water was being used by a firm in Germany.

SPECIMEN OUTLINE RECIPE.

Ingredients required for *plain eating-chocolate.*

Cacao nib or mass 33 parts. Cacao butter 13 " Sugar 53-3/4 " Flavouring 1/4 " ------------- 100 parts

Since eating-chocolate is produced by mixing sugar and cacao nib, with or without flavouring materials, and reducing to a fine homogeneous mass, the principles underlying its manufacture are obviously simple, yet when we come to consider the production of a modern high-class chocolate we find the processes involved are somewhat elaborate.

(a) *Preparing the Nib or "Mass."*

The nib is obtained in exactly the same way as in the manufacture of cocoa, the beans being cleaned, roasted and shelled. The roasting, however, is generally somewhat lighter for chocolate than for cocoa. The nibs produced may be used as they are, or they may be first ground to "mass" by means of mill-stones as described above.

(b) *Mixing in the Sugar.*

Some makers use clear crystalline granulated sugar, others disintegrate loaf sugar to a beautiful snow-white flour. The nib, coarse or finely ground, is mixed with the sugar in a kind of edge-runner or grinding-mixer, called a *mélangeur*. As is seen in the photo, the *mélangeur* consists of two heavy mill-stones which are supported on a granite floor. This floor revolves and causes the stationary mill-stones to rotate on their axes, so that although they run rapidly, like a man on a "joy wheel," they make no headway. The material is prevented from accumulating at the sides by curved scrapers, which gracefully deflect the stream of material to the part of the revolving floor which runs under the mill-stones. Thus the sugar and nib are mixed and crushed. As the mixture usually becomes like dough in consistency, it can be neatly removed from the *mélangeur* with a shovel. The operator rests a shovel lightly on the revolving floor, and the material mounts into a heap upon it.

[Illustration: CHOCOLATE MELANGEUR. Reproduced by permission of Messrs. Lake. Orr & Coy. Ltd.]

[Illustration: PLAN OF CHOCOLATE MELANGEUR.]

[Illustration: CHOCOLATE REFINING MACHINE. Reproduced by permission of Messrs. J. Baker & Sons, Willesden.]

(c) *Grinding the Mixture.*

The mixture is now passed through a mill, which has been described as looking like a multiple mangle. The object of this is to break down the sugar and cacao to smaller particles. The rolls may be made either of granite (more strictly speaking, of quartz diorite) or of polished chilled cast iron. Chilled cast iron rolls have the advantage that they can be kept cool by having water flowing through them. A skilled operator is required to set the rolls in order that they may give a large and satisfactory output. The cylinders in contact run at different speeds, and, as will be seen in the diagram, the chocolate always clings to the roll which is revolving with the greater velocity, and is delivered from the rolls either as a curtain of chocolate or as a spray of chocolate powder. It is very striking to see the soft chocolate-coloured dough become, after merely passing between the rolls, a dry powder--the explanation is that the sugar having been more finely crushed now requires a greater quantity of cacao butter to lubricate it before the mixture can again become plastic. The chocolate in its various stages of manufacture, should be kept warm or it will solidify and much time and heat (and possibly temper) will be absorbed in remelting it; for this and other reasons most chocolate factories have a number of hot rooms, in which the chocolate is stored whilst waiting to pass on to the next operation. The dry powder coming from the rolls is either taken to a hot room, or at once mixed in a warm *mélangeur*, where curiously enough the whole becomes once again of the consistency of dough. The grinding between the rolls and the mixing in the *mélangeur* are repeated any number of times until the chocolate is of the desired fineness. Whilst there are a few people who like the clean, hard feel of sugar crystals between the teeth, the present-day taste is all for very smooth and highly refined chocolate; hence the grinding operation is one of the most important in the factory, and is checked at the works at Bournville by measuring with a microscope the size of the particles. The cost of fine grinding is considerable, for whilst the first breaking down of the cacao nibs and sugar crystals is comparatively easy, it is found that as the particles of chocolate get finer the cost of further reduction increases by leaps and bounds. The chocolate may now proceed direct to the moulding rooms or it may first be conched.

[Illustration: GRINDING CACAO NIB AND SUGAR. (Messrs. Cadbury Bros., Bournville).]

[Illustration: SECTION THROUGH CHOCOLATE GRINDING ROLLS.]

(*d*) *Conching.*

We now come to an extraordinary process which is said to have been originally introduced to satisfy a fastidious taste that demanded a chocolate which readily melted in the mouth and yet had not the cloying effect which is produced by excess of cacao butter. In this process the chocolate is put in a vessel shaped something like a shell (hence called a *conche*), and a heavy roller is pushed to and fro in the chocolate. Although the conche is considered to have revolutionized the chocolate industry, it will remain to the uninitiated a curious sight to see a room full of machines engaged in pummelling chocolate day and night. There is no general agreement as to exactly how the conche produces its effects--from the scientific point of view the changes are complex and elusive, and too technical to explain here--but it is well known that if this process is continued for periods varying according to the result desired from a few hours to a week, characteristic changes occur which make the chocolate a more mellow and finished confection, having more or less the velvet feel of *chocolat fondant.*

(*e*) *Flavouring.*

Art is shown not only in the choice of the cacao beans but also in the selection of spices and essences, for, whilst the fundamental flavour of a chocolate is determined by the blend of beans and the method of manufacture, the piquancy and special character are often obtained by the addition of minute quantities of flavourings. The point in the manufacture at which the flavour is added is as late as possible so as to avoid the possible loss of aroma in handling. The flavours used include cardamom, cassia, cinnamon, cloves, coriander, lemon, mace, and last but most popular of all, the vanilla pod or vanillin. Some makers use the choice spices themselves, others prefer their essential oils. Many other nutty, fragrant and aromatic substances have been used; of these we may mention almonds, coffee, musk, ambergris, gum benzoin and balsam of Peru. The English like delicately flavoured confections, whilst the Spanish follow the old custom of heavily spicing the chocolate. In ancient recipes we read of the use of white and red peppers, and the addition of hot spices was defended and even recommended on purely philosophical grounds. It was given, in the strange jargon of the Peripatetics, as a dictum that chocolate is by nature cold and dry and therefore ought to be mixed with things which are hot.

[Illustration: "CONCHE" MACHINES. Reproduced by permission of Messrs. J. Baker & Sons, Willesden.]

[Illustration: SECTION THROUGH "CONCHE" MACHINE.]

[Illustration: MACHINES FOR MIXING OR "CONCHING" CHOCOLATE.]

(f) Moulding.

Small quantities of cacao butter will have been added to the chocolate at various stages, and hence the finished product is quite plastic. It is now brought from the hot room (or the *mélangeur* or the conche) to the moulding rooms. Before moulding, the chocolate is passed through a machine, known as a compressor, which removes air-bubbles. This is a necessary process, as people would not care to purchase chocolate full of holes. As in the previous operations, every effort has been made to produce a chocolate of smooth texture and fine flavour, so in the moulding rooms skill is exercised in converting the plastic mass into hard bars and cakes, which snap when broken and which have a pleasant appearance. Well-moulded chocolate has a good gloss, a rich colour and a correct shape.

[Illustration: CHOCOLATE SHAKING TABLE.]

The most important factor in obtaining a good appearance is the temperature, and chocolate is frequently passed through a machine (called a tempering machine) merely to give it the desired temperature. A suitable temperature for moulding, according to Zipperer, varies from 28° C. on a hot summer's day to 32° C. on a winter's day. As the melting point of cacao butter is about 32° C, it will be realized that the butter is super-cooled and is ready to crystallize on the slightest provocation. Each mould has to contain the same quantity of chocolate. Weighing by hand has been abandoned in favour of a machine which automatically deposits a definite weight, such as a quarter or half a pound, of the chocolate paste on each mould. The chocolate stands up like a lump of dough and has to be persuaded to lie down and fill the mould. This can be most effectively accomplished by banging the mould up and down on a table. In the factory the method used is to place the moulds on rocking tables which rise gradually and fall with a bump. The diagram will make clear how these vibrating tables are worked by means of ratchet wheels. Rocking tables are made which are silent in action, but the moulds jerkily dancing about on the table make a very lively clatter, such a noise as might be produced by a regiment of mad cavalry crossing a courtyard. During the shaking-up the chocolate fills every crevice of the mould, and any bubbles, which if left in would spoil the appearance of the chocolate, rise to the top. The chocolate then passes on to an endless band which conducts the mould through a chamber in which cold air is moving. As the chocolate cools, it solidifies and contracts so that it comes out of the mould clean and bright. In this way are produced the familiar sticks and cakes of chocolate. A similar method is used in producing "Croquettes" and the small tablets known as "Neapolitans." Other forms require more elaborate moulds; thus the chocolate eggs, which fill the confectioners' windows just before Easter, are generally hollow, unless they are very small, and are made in two halves by pressing chocolate in egg-shaped moulds and then uniting the two halves. Chocolate cremes, caramels, almonds and, in fact, fancy "chocolates" generally, are produced in quite a different manner. For these *chocolats de fantaisie* a rather liquid chocolate is required known as covering chocolate.

SPECIMEN OUTLINE RECIPE.

Ingredients required for *chocolate for covering cremes*, etc.:

Cacao nib or mass 30 parts Cacao butter 20 " Sugar 49-3/4 " Flavouring 1/4 " ------------- 100 parts

It is prepared in exactly the same way as ordinary eating chocolate, save that more butter is added to make it flow readily, so that in the melted condition it has about the same consistency as cream. The operations so far described are conducted by men, but the covering of cremes and the packing of the finished chocolates into boxes are performed by girls. Covering is light work requiring a delicate touch, and if, as is usual, it is done in bright airy rooms, is a pleasant occupation.

[Illustration: GIRLS COVERING, OR DIPPING, CREMES, ETC. (Messrs. Cadbury Bros., Bournville.)]

The girl sits with a small bowl of warm liquid chocolate in front of her, and on one side the "centres" (cremes, caramels, ginger, nuts, etc.) ready for covering with chocolate. The chocolate must be at just the right temperature, which is 88 °F., or 31° C. She takes one of the "centres," say a vanilla creme, on her fork and dips it beneath the chocolate. When she draws it out, the white creme is completely covered in brown chocolate and, without touching it with her finger, she deftly places it on a piece of smooth paper. A little twirl of the fork or drawing a prong across the chocolate will give the characteristic marking on the top of the chocolate creme. The chocolate rapidly sets to a crisp film enveloping the soft creme. There are in use in many chocolate factories some very ingenious covering machines, invented in 1903, which, as they clothe cremes in a robe of chocolate, are known as "enrobers"; it is doubtful, however, if the chocolates so produced have even quite so good an appearance as when the covering is done by hand.

[Illustration: THE ENROBER. A machine for covering cremes, etc., with chocolate. Reproduced by permission of Messrs. Savy Jeanjean & Co., Paris.]

It would be agreeable at this point to describe the making of cremes (which, by the way, contrary to the opinion of most writers, contain no cream or butter), and other products of the confectioner's art, but it would take us beyond the scope of the present book. We will only remind our readers of the great variety of comestibles and confections which are covered in chocolate--pistachio nut, roasted almonds, pralines, biscuits, walnuts, nougat, montelimar, fruits, fruit cremes, jellies, Turkish delight, marshmallows, caramels, pine-apple, noisette, and other delicacies.

[Illustration: A CONFECTIONERY ROOM AT MESSRS. CADBURY'S WORKS AT BOURNVILLE. Cutting almond paste by hand moulds.]

Milk Chocolate.

We owe the introduction of this excellent food and confection to the researches of M.D. Peter of Vevey, in Switzerland, who produced milk chocolate as early as 1876. Many of our older readers will remember their delight when in the eighteen nineties they first tasted Peter's milk chocolate. Later the then little firm of Cailler, realising the importance of having the factory on the very spot where rich milk was produced in abundance, established a works near Gruyères. This grew rapidly and soon became the largest factory in Switzerland. The sound principle of having your factory in the heart of a milk producing area was adopted by Cadbury's, who built milk condensing factories at the ancient village of Frampton-on-Severn, in Gloucestershire, and at Knighton, near Newport, Salop. Before the war these two factories together condensed from two to three million gallons of milk a year. Whilst the amount of milk used in England for making milk chocolate appears very great when expressed in gallons, it is seen to be very small (being only about one-half of one per cent.) when expressed as a fraction of the total milk production. Milk chocolate is not made from milk produced in the winter, when milk is scarce, but from milk produced in the spring and summer when there is milk in excess of the usual household requirements, and when it is rich and creamy. The importance of not interfering with the normal milk supply to local customers is appreciated by the chocolate makers, who take steps to prevent this. It will interest public analysts and others to know that Cadbury's have had no difficulty in making it a stipulation in their contracts with the vendors that the milk supplied to them shall contain at least 3.5 per cent. of butter fat, a 17 per cent. increase on the minimum fixed by the Government.

[Illustration: FACTORY AT FRAMPTON, GLOUCESTERSHIRE, AT WHICH MILK IS EVAPORATED FOR MILK CHOCOLATE MANUFACTURE. (Messrs. Cadbury Bros., Ltd.).]

SPECIMEN OUTLINE RECIPE.

Ingredients required for *milk chocolate*:

Cacao nib or mass (from 10 to 20 per cent.), say 10 Cacao Butter 20 Sugar 44-3/4 Milk solids (from 15 to 25 per cent.), say 25=(200 parts of milk.) Flavouring 1/4 -------- 100

Milk chocolate consists of an intimate mixture of cacao nib, sugar and milk, condensed by evaporation. The manner in which the milk is mixed with the cacao nib is a matter of taste, and the art of combining milk with chocolate, so as to retain the full flavour of each, has engaged the attention of many experts. At present there is no general method of manufacture--each maker has his own secret processes, which generally include the use of grinding mills, *mélangeurs*, conches, moulding machines, etc., as with plain chocolate. We cannot do better than refer those who wish to know more of this, or other branch of the chocolate industry, to the following English, French and German standard works on Chocolate Manufacture:

Cocoa and Chocolate, Their Chemistry and Manufacture, by R. Whymper (Churchill).

Fabrication du Chocolat, by Fritsch (Scientifique et Industrielle).

The Manufacture of Chocolate, by Dr. Paul Zipperer (Spon).

CHAPTER VII

BY-PRODUCTS OF THE COCOA AND CHOCOLATE
INDUSTRY

Of Cacao Butter.--

It is the best and most natural *Pomatum* for Ladies to *clear* and *plump* the Skin when it is *dry, rough*, or *shrivel'd*, without making it appear either *fat* or *shining*. The *Spanish Women* at *Mexico* use it very much, and it is highly esteem'd by them.

The Natural History of Chocolate, R. Brookes, 1730.

Of Cacao Shell.--

In Russia and Belgium many families take Caravello at breakfast. This is nothing but cocoa husk, washed and then boiled in milk.

Chocolate and Confectionery Manufacture, A. Jacoutot.

Cacao Butter.

In that very able compilation, *Allen's Organic Analysis*, Mr. Leonard Archbutt states (Vol. II, p. 176) that cacao butter "is obtained in large quantities as a by-product in the manufacture of chocolate." This is repeated in the excellent book on *Oils*, by C.A. Mitchell (Common Commodities of Commerce series). These statements are, of course, incorrect. We have seen that cacao butter is obtained as a by-product in the manufacture of cocoa, and is *consumed* in large quantities in the manufacture of chocolate. When, during the war, the use of sugar for chocolate-making was restricted and little chocolate was produced, the cacao butter formerly used in this industry was freed for other purposes. Thus there was plenty of cacao butter available at a time when other fats were scarce. Cacao butter has a pleasant, bland taste resembling cocoa. The cocoa flavour is very persistent, as many experimenters found to their regret in their efforts to produce a tasteless cacao butter which could be used as margarine or for general purposes in cooking. The scarcity of edible fats during the war forced the confectioners to try cacao butter, which in normal times is too expensive for them to use, and as a result a very large amount was employed in making biscuits and confectionery.

Cacao butter runs hot from the presses as an amber-coloured oil, and after nitration, sets to a pale golden yellow wax-like fat. The butter, which the pharmacist sells, is sometimes white and odourless, having been bleached and deodorized. The butter as produced is always pale yellow in colour, with a semi-crystalline or granular fracture and an agreeable taste and odour resembling cocoa or chocolate.

Cacao butter has such remarkable keeping properties (which would appear to depend on the aromatic substances which it contains), that a myth has arisen that it will keep for ever. The fable finds many believers even in scientific circles; thus W.H. Johnson, in the *Imperial Institute Handbook* on *Cocoa*, states that: "When pure, it has the peculiar property of not becoming rancid, however long it may be kept." Whilst this overstates the case, we find that under suitable conditions cacao butter will remain fresh and good for several years. Cacao butter has rather a low melting point (90° F.), so that whilst it is a hard, almost brittle, solid at ordinary temperatures, it melts readily when in contact with the human body (blood heat 98° F). This property, together with its remarkable stability, makes it useful for ointments, pomades, suppositories, pessaries and other pharmaceutical preparations; it also explains why actors have found it convenient for the removal of grease paint. The recognition of the value of cacao butter for cosmetic purposes dates from very early days; thus in Colmenero de Ledesma's

Curious Treatise on the Nature and Quality of Chocolate (printed at the Green Dragon, 1685), we read: "That they draw from the cacao a great quantity of butter, which they use to make their faces shine, which I have seen practised in the Indies by the Spanish women born there." This, evidently, was one way of shining in society.

Cacao butter has been put to many other uses, thus it has been employed in the preparation of perfumes, but the great bulk of the cacao butter produced is used up by the chocolate maker. For making chocolate it is ideal, and the demand for it for this purpose is so great that substitutes have been found and offered for sale. Until recently these fats, coconut stearine and others, could be ignored by the reputable chocolate makers as the confection produced by their use was inferior to true chocolate both in taste and in keeping properties. In recent times the oils and fats of tropical nuts and fruits have been thoroughly investigated in the eager search for new fats, and new substitutes, such as illipé butter, have been introduced, the properties of which closely resemble those of cacao butter.

For the information of chemists we may state that the analytical figures for genuine cacao butter, as obtained in the cocoa factory, are as follow:

ANALYTICAL FIGURES FOR CACAO BUTTER.

Specific Gravity (at 99° C. to water at 15.5° C.) .858 to .865 Melting Point 32°C. to 34°C. Titer (fatty acids) 49°C. to 50°C. Iodine Absorbed 34% to 38% Refraction (Butyro-Refractometer) at 40°C. 45.6° to 46.5° Saponification Value 192 to 198 Valenta 94°C. to 96°C. Reichert Meissel Value 1.0 Polenske Value 0.5 Kirschner " 0.5 Shrewsbury and Knapp Value 14 to 15 Unsaponifiable matter 0.3% to 0.8% Mineral matter 0.02% to 0.05% Acidity (as oleic acid) 0.6% to 2.0%

Although the trade in cacao butter is considerable, there were, before the war, only two countries that could really be considered as exporters of cacao butter; in other words, there were only two countries, namely, Holland and Germany, pressing out more cacao butter in the production of cocoa than they absorbed in making chocolate:

EXPORT OF CACAO BUTTER.

Tons (of 1000 kilogrammes) 1911 1912 1913 Holland 4,657 5,472 7,160 Germany 3,611 3,581 1,960 ----- ----- ----- 8,268 9,053 9,120 ----- ----- -----

During the war America appeared for the first time in her history as an exporter of cacao butter. Hitherto she was one of the principal importers, as will be seen in the following table:

IMPORTS OF CACAO BUTTER.

Tons (of 1000 kilogrammes) 1912 1913 United States 1,842 1,634 Switzerland 1,821 1,634 Belgium 1,127 1,197 Austria-Hungary 1,062 1,190 Russia 955 1,197 England 495 934

The next table shows the imports (expressed in English tons) into the United Kingdom in more recent years:

IMPORTS OF CACAO BUTTER.

Year 1912 1913 1914 1915 1916 1917 Tons 477 912 1512 599 962 675

The wholesale price of cacao butter has varied in the last six years from 1/3 per pound to 2/11 per pound, and was fixed in 1918 by the Food Controller at 1/6 per pound (retail price 2/- per pound). The control was removed in 1919, and immediately the wholesale price rose to 2/8 per pound.

Cacao Shell.

Although I have described cacao butter as a by-product, the only true by-product of the combined cocoa and chocolate industry is cacao shell. I explained in the previous chapter how it is separated from the roasted bean. As they come from the husking or winnowing machine, the larger fragments of shell resemble the shell of monkey-nuts (ground nuts or pea nuts), except that the cacao shells are thinner, more brittle and of a richer brown colour. The shell has a pleasant odour in which a little true cocoa aroma can be detected. The small pieces of shell look like bran, and, if the shell be powdered, the product is wonderfully like cocoa in appearance, though not in taste or smell. As the raw cacao bean contains on the average about twelve and a half per cent. of shell, it is evident that the world production must be considerable (about 36,000 tons a year), and since it is not legitimately employed in cocoa, the brains of inventors have been busy trying to find a use for it. In some industries the by-product has proved on investigation to be of greater value than the principal product--a good instance of this is glycerine as a by-product in soap manufacture--but no use for the husk or shell of cacao, which gives it any considerable commercial value, has yet been discovered. There are signs, however, that its possible uses are being considered and appreciated.

For years small quantities of cacao shell, under the name of "miserables," have been used in Ireland and other countries for producing a dilute infusion for drinking. Although this "cocoa tea" is not unpleasant, and has mild stimulating properties, it has never been popular, and even during the war, when it was widely advertised and sold in England under fancy names at fancy prices, it never had a large or enthusiastic body of consumers.

In normal times the cocoa manufacturer has no difficulty in disposing of his shell to cattle-food makers and others, but during 1915 when the train service was so defective, and transport by any other means almost impossible, the manufacturers of cocoa and chocolate were unable to get the shell away from their factories, and had large accumulations of it filling up valuable store space. In these circumstances they attempted to find a use near at hand. It was tried with moderate success as a fuel and a considerable quantity was burned in a special type of gas-producer intended for wood.

Cacao shell has a high nitrogenous content, and if burned yields about 67 lbs. of potassium carbonate per ton. In the Annual Report of the Experimental Farms in Canada, (1898, p. 151 and 1899, p. 851,) accounts are given of the use of cacao shell as a manure. The results given are encouraging, and experiments were made at Bournville. At first these were only moderately successful, because the shell is extremely stable and decomposes in the ground very slowly indeed. Then the head gardener tried hastening the decomposition by placing the shell in a heap, soaking with water and turning several times before use. In this way the shell was converted into a decomposing mass before being applied to the ground, and gave excellent results both as a manure and as a lightener of heavy soils.

On the Continent the small amount of cacao butter which the shell contains is extracted from it by volatile solvents. The "shell butter" so obtained is very inferior to ordinary cacao butter, and as usually put on the market, has an unpleasant taste, and an odour which reminds one faintly of an old tobacco-pipe. In this unrefined condition it is obviously unsuitable for edible purposes.

Shell contains about one per cent. of *theobromine* (dimethylxanthine). This is a very valuable chemical substance (see remarks in chapter on Food Value of Cocoa and Chocolate), and the extraction of theobromine from shell is already practised on a large scale, and promises to be a profitable industry. Ordinary commercial samples of shell contain from 1.2 to 1.4 per cent. of theobromine. Those interested should study the very ingenious process of Messrs. Grousseau and Vicongne (Patent No. 120,178). Many other uses of cacao shell have been made and suggested; thus it has been used for the production of a good coffee substitute, and also, during the shortage of sawdust, as a packing material, but its most important use at the present time is as cattle food, and its most important abuse as an adulterant of cocoa.

The value of cacao shell as cattle food has been known for a long time, and is indicated in the following analysis by Smetham (in the Journal of the Lancashire Agricultural Society, 1914).

ANALYSIS OF CACAO SHELL.

Water 9.30 Fat 3.83 Mineral Matter 8.20 Albuminoids 18.81 Fibre 13.85 Digestible Carbohydrates 46.01 ------ 100.00 ------

From these figures Smetham calculates the food units as 102, so that it is evident that cacao shell occupies a good position when compared with other fodders:

FOOD UNITS.

Linseed cake 133 Oatmeal 117 Bran 109 English wheat 106 *Cacao shells* 102 Maize (new crop) 99 Meadow hay 68 Rice husks 43 Wheat straw 41 Mangels 12

These analytical results have been supported by practical feeding experiments in America and Germany (see full account in Zipperer's book, *The Manufacture of Chocolate*). Prof. Faelli, in Turin, obtained, by giving cacao shell to cows, an increase in both the quantity and quality of the milk. More recent experience seems to indicate that it is unwise to put a very high percentage of cacao shell in a cattle food; in small quantities in compound feeding cakes, etc., as an appetiser it has been used for years with good results. (Further particulars will be found in *Cacao Shells as Fodder*, by A.W. Knapp, *Tropical Life*, 1916, p. 154, and in *The Separation and Uses of Cacao Shell*, Society of Chemical Industry's Journal, 1918, 240). The price of shell has shown great variation. The following figures are for the grade of shell which is almost entirely free from cocoa:

CACAO SHELL.

AVERAGE PRICE PER TON.

Year 1912 1913 1914 1915 1916 1917 1918 1919 Price 65/- 70/- 70/- 70/- 90/- 128/- 284/- 161/-

PRICE PER FOOD UNIT.

July, 1915. *Jan.*, 1919. *s. d. s. d.* English Oats 3 1-1/2 3 8 Cotton Seed Cake 2 5 3 11 Linseed Cake 1 7 3 5 Brewers Grains (dried) 1 6-1/2 3 8-1/2 Decorticated Cotton Cake 1 6 3 3-1/2 Cacao Shell 8-1/4 1 4-1/2

The above table speaks for itself; the figures are from the Journal of the Board of Agriculture; I have added cacao shell for comparison.

CHAPTER VIII

THE COMPOSITION AND FOOD VALUE OF COCOA AND
CHOCOLATE

Before the Spaniards made themselves Masters of Mexico, no
other drink was esteem'd but that of cocoa; none caring for wine,
notwithstanding the soil produces vines everywhere in great
abundance of itself.

John Ogilvy's *America*, 1671.

The early writers on chocolate generally became lyrical when
they wrote of its value as a food. Thus in the *Natural History of
Chocolate*, by R. Brookes (1730), we read that an ounce of
chocolate contains as much nourishment as a pound of beef,
that a woman and a child, and even a councillor, lived on
chocolate alone for a long period, and further: "Before chocolate
was known in Europe, good old wine was called the milk of old
men; but this title is now applied with greater reason to
chocolate, since its use has become so common, that it has
been perceived that chocolate is, with respect to them, what milk
is to infants."

A more temperate tone is shown in the following, from *A Curious
Treatise of the Nature and Quality of Chocolate*, by Antonio
Colmenero de Ledesma, a Spaniard, Physician and Chyrurgion
of the city of Ecija, in Andaluzia (printed at the Green Dragon,
1685):

So great is the number of those persons, who at present do drink
of Chocolate, that not only in the West Indies, whence this drink
has its original and beginning, but also in Spain, Italy, Flanders,
&c., it is very much used, and especially in the Court of the King
of Spain; where the great ladies drink it in a morning before they
rise out of their beds, and lately much used in England, as Diet

and Phisick with the Gentry. Yet there are several persons that stand in doubt both of the hurt and of the benefit, which proceeds from the use thereof; some saying, that it obstructs and causes opilations, others and those the most part, that it fattens, several assure us that it fortifies the stomach: some again that it heats and inflames the body. But very many steadfastly affirm, that tho' they shou'd drink it at all hours, and that even in the Dog-days, they find themselves very well after it.

So much for the old valuations; let us now attempt by modern methods to estimate the food value of cacao and its preparations.

Food Value of Cacao Beans.

In estimating the worth of a food, it is usual to compare the fuel values. This peculiar method is adopted because the most important requirement in nutrition is that of giving energy for the work of the body, and a food may be thought of as being burnt up (oxidised) in the human machine in the production of heat and energy. The various food constituents serve in varying degrees as fuel to produce energy, and hence to judge of the food value it is necessary to know the chemical composition. Below we give the average composition of cacao beans and the fuel value calculated from these figures:

AVERAGE COMPOSITION AND FUEL VALUE OF FRESHLY ROASTED CACAO BEANS (NIBS).

Composition. Energy-giving power Calories per lb.

Cacao Butter 54.0 = 2,282 Protein (total nitrogen 2.3%) 11.9 = 221 Cacao Starch 6.7 } = 472 Other Digestible Carbohydrates, etc. 18.7 } Stimulants { Theobromine 1.0 { Caffein 0.4 Mineral Matter 3.2 Crude Fibre 2.6 Moisture 1.5 ------ ----- 100.0 2,975

------ -----

[Illustration: COCOA AND CHOCOLATE DESPATCH DECK AT BOURNVILLE.]

It will be seen from the above analysis that the cacao bean is rich in fats, carbohydrates and protein, and that it contains small quantities of the two stimulants, theobromine and caffein. In the whole range of animal and vegetable foodstuffs there are only one or two which exceed it in energy-giving power. If expressed in quite another way, namely, as "food units," the value of the cacao bean stands equally high, as is shown by the following figures taken from Smetham's result published in the Journal of the Royal Agricultural Society, 1914:

"FOOD UNITS."

Turnips 8 Carrots 12 Potatoes 26 Rice 102 Corn Flour 104 Wheat 106 Peas 113 Oatmeal 117 Coconut 159 Cacao Bean 183

These figures indicate the high food value of the raw material; we will now proceed to consider the various products which are obtained from it.

Food Value of Cocoa.

AVERAGE COMPOSITION AND FUEL VALUE OF UNTREATED COCOA.

Composition. Energy-giving power Calories per lb.

Cacao Butter 28.0 = 1,183 Protein 18.3 = 340 Cacao Starch 10.2 } = 718 Other Digestible Carbohydrates, etc. 28.4 } Stimulants {Theobromine 1.5 {Caffein 0.6 Mineral Matter 5.0 Crude Fibre 4.0 Moisture 4.0 ----- ----- 100.0 2,241 ----- -----

("Soluble" Cocoa, *i.e.*, cocoa which has been treated with alkaline salts, is almost identical in composition, save that the mineral matter is about 7.5 per cent.).

As cocoa consists of the cacao bean with some of the butter extracted--a process which increases the percentage of the nitrogenous and carbohydrate constituents--it will be evident that the food value of cocoa powder is high, and that it is a concentrated foodstuff. In this respect it differs from tea and coffee, which have practically no food value; each of them, however, have special qualities of their own. Some of the claims made for these beverages are a little remarkable. The Embassy of the United Provinces in their address to the Emperor of China (Leyden, 1655), in mentioning the good properties of tea, wrote: "More especially it disintoxicates those that are fuddl'd, giving them new forces, and enabling them to go to it again." The Embassy do not state whether they speak from personal experience, but their admiration for tea is undoubted. Tea, coffee, and cocoa are amongst our blessings, each has its devotees, each has its peculiar delight: tea makes for cheerfulness, coffee makes for wit and wakefulness, and cocoa relieves the fatigued, and gives a comfortable feeling of satisfaction and stability. Of these three drinks cocoa alone can be considered as a food, and just as there are people whose digestion is deranged by tea, and some who sleep not a wink after drinking coffee, so there are some who find cocoa too feeding, especially in the summer-time. These sufferers from biliousness will think it curious that cocoa is habitually drunk in many hot climates, thus, in Spanish-speaking countries, it is the custom for the priest, after saying mass, to take a cup of chocolate. The pure cocoa powder is, as we saw above, a very rich foodstuff, but it must always be remembered that in a pint of cocoa only a small quantity, about half an ounce, is usually taken. In this connection the following comparison between tea, coffee and cocoa is not without interest. It is taken from the *Farmer's Bulletin* 249, an official publication of the United States

Department of Agriculture:

COMPARISON OF ENERGY-GIVING POWER OF A PINT OF TEA, COFFEE AND COCOA.

Fuel value Kind of Beverage Water Protein Fat Carbohydrates per lb. ---
% % % % Calories *Tea* (0.5 oz. to 1 pt. water) 99.5 0.2 0 0.6 15 *Coffee* (1 oz. to 1 pt. water) 98.9 0.2 0 0.7 16 *Cocoa* (0.5 oz. to 1 pt. water) 97.1 0.6 0.9 1.1 65

These figures place cocoa, as a food, head and shoulders above tea and coffee. The figures are for the beverages made without the addition of milk and sugar, both of which are almost invariably present. A pint of cocoa made with one-third milk, half an ounce of cocoa, and one ounce of sugar would have a fuel value of 320 calories, and is therefore equivalent in energy-giving power to a quarter of a pound of beef or four eggs.

Cocoa is stimulating, but its action is not so marked as that of tea or coffee, and hence it is more suitable for young children. Dr. Hutchison, an authority on dietetics, writes: "Tea and coffee are also harmful to the susceptible nervous system of the child, but cocoa, made with plenty of milk, may be allowed, though it should be regarded, like milk, as a food rather than a beverage properly so called."

How to Make a Cup of Cocoa.

Tea, coffee and cocoa are all so easy to make that it is remarkable anyone should fail to prepare them perfectly. Whilst in France everyone can prepare coffee to perfection, and many fail in making a cup of tea, in England all are adepts in the art of tea-making, and many do not distinguish themselves in the preparation of coffee. Cocoa in either country is not always the delightful beverage it should be. The directions below, if carefully followed, will be found to give the character of cocoa its full expression. The principal conditions to observe are to avoid iron saucepans, to use boiling water or milk, to froth the cocoa before serving, and to serve steaming hot in thick cups.

[Illustration]

The amount of cocoa required for two large breakfast cups, that is one pint, is as much as will go, when piled up, in a dessert spoon. Take then a heaped dessert-spoonful of pure cocoa and mix dry with one and a half times its bulk of fine sugar. Set this on one side whilst the boiling liquid is prepared. Mix one breakfast cup of water with one breakfast cup of milk, and raise to the boil in an enamelled saucepan. Whilst this is proceeding, warm the jug which is to hold the cocoa, and transfer the dry sugar-cocoa mixture to it. Now pour in the boiling milk and water. Transfer back to saucepan and *boil* for one minute. Whisk vigorously for a quarter of a minute. Serve without delay.

Digestibility of Cocoa.

We have noted above the high percentage of nutrients which cocoa contains, and the research conducted by J. Forster[1] shows that these nutrients are easily assimilated. Forster found that the fatty and mineral constituents of cocoa are both *completely* digested, and the nitrogenous constituents are digested in the same proportion as in finest bread, and more completely than in bread of average quality. One very striking fact was revealed by his researches, namely, that the consumption of cocoa increases the digestive power for other foods which are taken at the same time, and that this increase is particularly evident with milk. Dr. R.O. Neumann[2] (who fed himself with cocoa preparations for over twelve weeks), whilst not agreeing with this conclusion, states that: "The consumption of cocoa from the point of view of health leaves nothing to be desired. The taking of large or small quantities of cocoa, either rich or poor in fat, with or without other food, gave rise to no digestive troubles during the 86 days which formed the duration of the experiments." He considers that cocoas containing a high percentage of cacao butter are preferable to those which contain low percentages, and that a 30 per cent. butter content meets all requirements. It is worthy of note that 28 to 30 per cent. is the quantity of butter found in ordinary high-class cocoas.

[1] *Hygienische Rundschau*, 1900, p. 305.

[2] *Die Bewertung des Kakaos als Nahrungs- und Genussmittel*, 1906.

As experts are liable to disagree, and it is almost possible to prove anything by a judicious selection from their writings, it may be well to give an extract from some modern text book as more nearly expressing the standard opinion of the times. In *Second Stage Hygiene*, by Mr. Ikin and Dr. Lyster, a text book written for the Board of Education Syllabus, we read, p. 96: "... in the better cocoas the greater part of the fat is removed by heat and pressure. In this form cocoa may be looked upon as almost an ideal food, as it contains proteids, fats, and carbohydrates in roughly the right proportions. Prepared with milk and sugar it forms a highly nutritious and valuable stimulating beverage."

Stimulating Property of Cocoa.

The mild stimulating property which cocoa possesses is due to the presence of the two substances, theobromine and caffein. The presence of theobromine is peculiar to cocoa, but caffein is a stimulating principle which also occurs in tea and coffee. Whilst in the quantities in which they are present in cocoa (about 1.5 per cent. of theobromine and 0.6 per cent. of caffein) they act only as agreeable stimulants, in the pure condition, as white crystalline powders, they are powerful curative agents. Caffein is well known as a specific for nervous headaches, and as a heart stimulant and diuretic. Theobromine is similar in action, but has the advantage for certain cases, that it has much less effect on the central nervous system, and for this reason it is a very valuable medicine for sufferers from heart dropsy, and as a tonic for senile heart. That its medicinal properties are appreciated is shown by its price: during 1918 the retail price was about 8 shillings an ounce, from which we can calculate that every pound of cocoa contained nearly two shillingsworth of theobromine.

"Soluble" Cocoa.

Whilst Forster states that treated cocoa is the most digestible, experts are not in agreement as to which is the more valuable foodstuff, the pure untouched cocoa, or that which is treated during its manufacture with alkaline salts. The cocoa so treated is generally described as "soluble," although its only claim to this name is that the mineral salts in the cocoa are rendered more soluble by the treatment. It is also sometimes incorrectly described as containing alkali, but actually no alkali is present in the cocoa either in a free state or as carbonate; the potassium exists "in the form of phosphates or combinations of organic acids, that is to say, in the ideal form in which these bodies occur in foods of animal and vegetable origin" (Fritsch, *Fabrication du Chocolat*, p. 216).

[Illustration: BOXING CHOCOLATES.]

Food Value of Chocolate.

I ate a little chocolate from my supply, well knowing the miraculous sustaining powers of the simple little block (from *Mr. Isaacs*, by F. Marion Crawford).

Whilst the food value of cocoa powder is very high the drink prepared from it can only be regarded as an accessory food, because it is usual to take the powder in small quantities--just as with beef-tea it is usual to take only a small portion of an ox in a tea-cup--but chocolate is often eaten in considerable quantities at a time, and must therefore be regarded as an important foodstuff, and not considered, as it frequently is considered, simply as a luxury.

The eating of cacao mixed with sugar dates from very early days, but it is only in recent times that it has become the principal sweetmeat. What would a "sweetshop" be to-day without chocolate, that summit of the confectioner's art, when the rich brown of chocolate is the predominant note in every confectioner's window? What would the lovers in England do without chocolates, which enable them to indulge their delight in giving that which is sure to be well received?

As a luxury it is universally appreciated, and because of this appreciation its value as a food is sometimes overlooked.

During the war chocolate was valued as a compact foodstuff, which is easily preserved. Dr. Gastineau Earle, lecturing for the Institute of Hygiene in 1915 on "Food Factor in War," said: "Chocolate is a most valuable concentrated food, especially when other foods are not available; it is the chief constituent of the emergency ration." Its importance as a concentrated foodstuff was appreciated in the United States, for every "comfort kit" made up for the American soldiers fighting in the war contained a cake of sweet chocolate.

There are a number of records of people whose lives have been preserved by means of chocolate. One of the most recent was the case of Commander Stewart, who was torpedoed in H.M.S. "Cornwallis" in the Mediterranean in 1917. He happened to have in his cabin one of the boxes of chocolate presented to the Army and Navy in 1915 by the colonies of Trinidad, Grenada, and St. Lucia, who gave the cacao and paid English manufacturers to make it into chocolate. He had been treasuring the box as a souvenir, but being the only article of food available, he filled his pockets with the chocolate, which sustained him through many trying hours.[3]

[3] See *West India Committee Journal*, p. 55, 1917.

We have already seen the high food value of the cacao bean: what of the sugar which chocolate contains? Sugar is consumed in large quantities in England, the consumption per head amounting to 80-90 lbs. per year. It is well known as a giver of heat and energy, and Sir Ernest Shackleton reports that it proved a great life preserver and sustainer in Arctic regions. Our practical acquaintance with sugar commences at birth--milk containing about 5 per cent. of milk sugar--and when one considers the amazing activity of young children one understands their continuous demand for sugar. Dr. Hutchison, in his well-known *Food and the Principles of Dietetics*, says: "The craving for sweets which children show is, no doubt, the natural expression of a physiological need, but they should be taken with, and not between, meals. Chocolate is one of the most wholesome and nutritious forms of such sweets."

Both the constituents of chocolate being nourishing, it follows that chocolate itself has a high food value. This is proved by the figures given below.

As with cocoa, we have first to know the composition before we can calculate the food value. The relative proportions of nib, butter and sugar, vary considerably in ordinary chocolate, so that it is difficult to give an average composition: there are sticks of eating chocolate which contain as little as 24 per cent. of cacao butter, whilst chocolate used for covering contains about 36 per cent. of butter.

As modern high-class eating chocolate contains about 31 per cent. of butter, we will take this for purposes of calculation:

AVERAGE COMPOSITION AND FUEL VALUE OF ENGLISH EATING CHOCOLATE.

Composition Energy-giving power

Calories per lb. Cacao Butter 31.4 = 1,327 Protein (total nitrogen 0.78%) 4.1 = 76 Cacao Starch 2.3 } = 162 Other Digestible Carbohydrates, etc. 6.4 } Stimulants { Theobromine 0.3 { Caffein 0.1 Mineral Matter 1.2 Crude Fibre 0.9 Moisture 1.0 Sugar 52.3 = 973 ----- ----- 100.0 2,538

In Snyder's *Human Foods* (1916) the official analyses of 163 common foods are given. They include practically everything that human beings eat, and only three are greater than chocolate in energy-giving power.

The result (2,538 calories per lb.) which we obtain by calculation is lower than the figure (2,768 calories per lb.) for chocolate given by Sherman in his book on *Food and Nutrition* (1918). Probably his figure is for unsweetened chocolate. The table below shows the energy-giving value of cocoa and chocolate compared with well-known foodstuffs. The figures (save for "eating" chocolate) are taken from Sherman's book, and are calculated from the analyses given in Bulletin 28 of the United States Department of Agriculture:

FUEL VALUE OF FOODSTUFFS.

Foodstuff as Calories Purchased. *per lb.* Cabbage 121 Cod Fish 209 Apples 214 Potatoes 302 Milk 314 Eggs 594 Beef Steak 960 Bread (average white) 1,180 Oatmeal 1,811 Sugar 1,815 Cocoa 2,258 Eating Chocolate 2,538

[Illustration: PACKING CHOCOLATES AT BOURNVILLE.]

Food Value of Milk Chocolate.

The value of milk as a food is so generally recognised as to need no commendation here. When milk is evaporated to a dry solid, about 87.5 per cent. of water is driven off, so that the dry milk left has about eight times the food value of the original milk. Milk chocolate of good quality contains from 15 to 25 per cent. of milk solids. Milk chocolate varies greatly in composition, but for the purpose of calculating the food value, we may assume that about a quarter of a high-class milk chocolate consists of solid milk, and this is combined with about 40 per cent. of cane sugar and 35 per cent. of cacao butter and cacao mass.

ANALYSIS AND FUEL VALUE OF MILK CHOCOLATE.

Energy-giving power. Calories per lb.

Milk Fat and Cacao Butter 35.0 = 1,480 Milk and Cocoa Proteins 8.0 = 149 Cacao Starch and Digestible Carbohydrates 3.0 = 56 Stimulants (Theobromine and Caffein) 0.2 Mineral Matter 2.0 Crude Fibre 0.3 Moisture 1.5 Milk Sugar and Cane Sugar 50.0 = 930 ----- ----- 100.0 = 2,615 ----- -----

It will be noted that the food value of milk chocolate is even greater than that of plain chocolate. It is highly probable that milk chocolate is the most nutritious of all sweetmeats. It is not generally recognised that when we purchase one pound of high-class milk chocolate we obtain three-quarters of a pound of chocolate and two pounds of milk!

CHAPTER IX

ADULTERATION AND THE NEED FOR DEFINITIONS

Those that mix maize in the Chocolate do very ill, for they beget bilious and melancholy humours.

A Curious Treatise on the Nature and Quality of Chocolate, Antonio Colmenero de Ledesma, 1685.

COCOA.

Cocoa might conveniently be defined as consisting exclusively of shelled, roasted, finely-ground cacao beans, partially de-fatted, with or without a minute quantity of flavouring material.

The gross adulteration of cocoa is now a thing of the past, and most of the cocoa sold conforms with this definition. Statements, however, get copied from book to book, and hence we continue to read that cocoa usually contains arrowroot or other starch. In the old days this was frequently so, but now, owing to many legal actions by Public Health Authorities, this abuse has been stamped out. Nowadays if a Public Analyst finds flour or arrowroot in a sample bought as cocoa, he describes it as adulterated, and the seller is prosecuted and fined. Hence, save for the presence of cacao shell, the cocoa of the present day is a pure article consisting simply of roasted, finely-ground cacao beans partially de-fatted. The principal factors affecting the quality of the finished cocoa are the difference in the kind of cacao bean used, the amount of cacao butter extracted, the care in preparation, and the amount of cacao shell left in.

The presence of more than a small percentage of shell in cocoa is a disadvantage both on the ground of taste and of food value. This has been recognised from the earliest times (see quotations on p. 128). In the Cocoa Powder Order of 1918, the amount of shell which a cocoa powder might contain was defined--*grade A* not to contain more than two per cent. of shell, and *grade B* not more than five per cent. of shell. The manufacturers of high-class cocoa welcomed these standards, but unfortunately the known analytical methods are not delicate enough to estimate accurately such small quantities, so that any external check is difficult, and the purchaser has to trust to the honesty of the manufacturer. Hence it is wise to purchase cocoa only from makers of good repute.

CHOCOLATE.

We have so far no legal definition of chocolate in England. As Mr. N.P. Booth pointed out at the Seventh International Congress of Applied Chemistry: "At the present time a mixture of cocoa with sugar and starch cannot be sold as pure cocoa, but only as 'chocolate powder,' and with a definite declaration that the article is a mixture of cocoa and other ingredients. Prosecutions are constantly occurring where mixtures of foreign starch and sugar with cocoa have been sold as 'cocoa,' and it seems, therefore, a proper step to take to require that a similar declaration shall be made in the case of 'chocolate' which contains other constituents than the products of cocoa nib and sugar." We cannot do better than quote in full the definitions suggested in Mr. Booth's paper.

The author refers to the absence of any legal standard for chocolate in England, although in some of the European countries standards are in force, and points out, as a result of this, that articles of which the sale would be prohibited in some other countries, are permitted to come without restriction on to the English market.

[Illustration: WHARF AT FACTORY AT KNIGHTON, AT WHICH MILK IS EVAPORATED FOR MILK CHOCOLATE MANUFACTURE. (Messrs. Cadbury Bros., Ltd.)]

He suggests that the following definitions for chocolate goods are reasonable, and could be conformed to by makers of the genuine article. These standards are not more stringent than those already enforced in some of the Colonies and European countries:

(1) Unsweetened chocolate or *cacao mass* must be prepared exclusively from roasted, shelled, finely-ground cacao beans, with or without the addition of a small quantity of flavouring matter, and should not contain less than 45 per cent. of cacao butter.

(2) Sweetened chocolate or *chocolate*.--A preparation consisting exclusively of the products of roasted, shelled, finely-ground cacao beans, and not more than 65 per cent. of sugar, with or without a small quantity of harmless flavouring matter.

(3) *Granulated*, or *Ground Chocolate for Drinking* purposes.--The same definition as for sweetened chocolate should apply here, except that the proportion of sugar may be raised to not more than 75 per cent.

(4) *Chocolate-covered Goods.*--Various forms of confectionery covered with chocolate, the composition of the latter agreeing with the definition of sweetened chocolate.

(5) *Milk Chocolate.*--A preparation composed exclusively of roasted, shelled cacao beans, sugar, and not less than 15 per cent. of the dry solids of full-cream milk, with or without a small quantity of harmless flavouring matter.

Mr. Booth further states that starch other than that naturally present in the cacao bean, and cacao shell in powder form, should be absolutely excluded from any article which is to be sold under the name of "chocolate."

CHAPTER X

THE CONSUMPTION OF CACAO

The Kernels that come to us from the Coast of *Caraqua*, are more oily, and less bitter, than those that come from the *French* Islands, and in *France* and *Spain* they prefer them to these latter. But in *Germany* and in the *North* (*Fides sit penes autorem*) they have a quite opposite Taste. Several People mix that of *Caraqua* with that of the Islands, half in half, and pretend by this Mixture to make the Chocolate better. I believe in the bottom, the difference of Chocolates is not considerable, since they are only obliged to increase or diminish the Proportion of Sugar, according as the Bitterness of the Kernels require it.

The Natural History of Chocolate, R. Brookes, 1730.

The war has caused such a disturbance that the statistics for the years of the war are difficult to obtain. For many years the German publication, the *Gordian*, was the most reliable source of cacao statistics, and so far we have nothing in England sufficiently comprehensive to replace it, although useful figures can be obtained from the Board of Trade returns of imports into Great Britain, from Mr. Theo. Vasmer's reports which appear from time to time in *The Confectioners' Union* and elsewhere, from Mr. Hamel Smith's collated material in *Tropical Life*, and from the reports of important brokers like Messrs. Woodhouse. In 1919 the *Bulletin of the Imperial Institute* gave a very complete *résumé* of cacao production as far as the British Empire is concerned.

Great Britain.

Since 1830 the consumption of cacao in the British Isles has shown a great and continuous increase, and there is every reason to believe that the consumption will easily keep pace with the rapidly growing production. One effect of the war has been to increase the consumption of cocoa and chocolate. Many thousands of men who took no interest in "sweets" learned from the use of their emergency ration that chocolate was a very convenient and concentrated foodstuff.

CACAO BEANS CLEARED FOR HOME CONSUMPTION.

Year. English Tons. 1830 450 1840 900 1850 1,400 1860 1,450 1870 3,100 1880 4,700 1890 9,000 1900 16,900 1910 24,550

CACAO BEANS IMPORTED INTO UNITED KINGDOM.

Total Retained in *Home Year. Imported* the country *Consumption* tons. tons. tons. 1912 33,600 27,450 24,600 1913 35,000 28,200 23,200 1914 41,750 29,600 24,900 1915 81,800 54,400 40,300 1916 88,800 64,750 29,300 1917 57,900 53,100 41,300

The above figures are compiled from the *Bulletin of the Imperial Institute* (No. 1, 1919). The total imports for 1918 were 42,390 tons. This sudden and marked drop in the amount imported was due to shortage of shipping. There were, however, large quantities of cacao in stock, and the amount consumed showed a marked advance on previous years, being 61,252 tons.

The Board of Trade Returns for 1919 are as follow:

CACAO BEANS IMPORTED INTO UNITED KINGDOM.

From British West Africa 72,886 tons British West Indies 13,219 tons Ecuador 9,153 tons Brazil 3,665 tons Ceylon 903 tons Other Countries 13,820 tons ------------ Total 113,646 tons ------------ Home Consumption 64,613 tons

It will be noted that the import of British cacao is over 75 per cent. of the total.

Before the war about half the cacao imported into the United Kingdom was grown in British possessions. During the war more and more British cacao was imported, and now that a preferential duty of seven shillings per hundredweight has been given to British Colonial growths we shall probably see a still higher percentage of British cacao consumed in the United Kingdom.

VALUE OF CACAO BEANS IMPORTED INTO THE UNITED KINGDOM (TO NEAREST £1,000).

Total value of Cacao From British Possessions. Year. Beans Imported. *Value. Per cent.* 1913 £2,199,000 £1,158,000 52.7 1914 £2,439,000 £1,204,000 49.4 1915 £5,747,000 £3,546,000 61.7 1916 £6,498,000 £4,417,000 68.0 1917 £3,498,000 £3,010,000 86.0 1918 £3,040,000 £2,549,000 83.8 1919 £9,207,000 £6,639,000 72.1

That the consumption of cacao is expected to grow greater yet in the immediate future is reflected in the prices of raw cacao, which, as soon as they were no longer fixed by the Government, rose rapidly, thus Accra cacao rose from 65s. per hundredweight to over 90s. per hundredweight in a few weeks, and now (January, 1920) stands at 104s. (See diagram p. 113).

World Consumption.

The world's consumption of cacao is steadily rising. Before the war the United States, Germany, Holland, Great Britain, France, and Switzerland were the principal consumers. Whilst we have increased our consumption, so that Great Britain now occupies second place, the United States has outstripped all the other countries, having doubled its consumption in a few years, and is now taking almost as much as all the rest of the world put together. It is thought that since America has "gone dry" this remarkably large consumption is likely to be maintained.

WORLD'S CONSUMPTION OF CACAO BEANS. (to the nearest thousand tons) 1 ton = 1000 kilograms.

Pre-war War Period Post-war

Average of 1913. 1914, 5, 6,& 7. 1918. 1919. Country. Tons. Tons. Tons. Tons.

Country	Pre-war Average of 1913. Tons.	War Period 1914, 5, 6,& 7. Tons.	1918. Tons.	Post-war 1919. Tons.
U.S.A.	68,000	103,000	145,000	145,000
Germany	51,000	28,000	?	13,000
Holland	30,000	25,000	2,000	39,000
Great Britain	28,000	41,000	62,000	66,000
France	28,000	35,000	39,000	46,000
Switzerland	10,000	14,000	18,000	21,000
Austria	7,000	2,000	?	2,000
Belgium	6,000	1,000	1,000	8,000
Spain	6,000	7,000	6,000	8,000
Russia	5,000	4,000	?	?
Canada	3,000	4,000	9,000	?
Italy	2,000	5,000	6,000	6,000
Denmark	2,000	2,000	2,000	?
Sweden	1,000	2,000	2,000	?
Norway	1,000	2,000	2,000	?
Other countries (estimated)	5,000	8,000	11,000	26,000
Total	252,000	283,000	305,000	380,000

The above figures are compiled chiefly from Mr. Theo. Vasmer's reports. The *Gordian* estimates that the world's consumption in 1918 was 314,882 tons. In several of our larger colonies and in at least one European country there is obviously ample room for increase in the consumption. When one considers the great population of Russia, four to five thousand tons per annum is a very small amount to consume. It is pleasant to think of cocoa being drunk in the icebound North of Russia--it brings to mind so picturesque a contrast: cacao, grown amongst the richly-coloured flora of the tropics, consumed in a land that is white with cold. When Russia has reached a more stable condition we shall doubtless see a rapid expansion in the cacao consumption.

[Illustration: CACAO PODS, LEAVES AND FLOWERS. Reproduced by permission of Messrs. Fry & Sons, Ltd., Bristol.]

BIBLIOGRAPHY

BOOKS ON COCOA AND CHOCOLATE ARRANGED IN ORDER OF DATE OF PUBLICATION.

1600-1700

RAUCH, Joan. Franc.

DISPUTATIO MEDICO DIOETETICA DE AËRE ET ESCULENTIS, DE NECNON POTU. Vienna 1624

[Condemns cocoa as a violent inflamer of the passions.]

COLMENERO, Antonio de Ledesma.

[Treatise on Chocolate in Spanish entitled:] CURIOSO TRATADO DE LA NATURALEZA Y CALIDAD DEL CHOCOLATE, DIVIDIDO EN QUATRO PUNTOS. Madrid 1631

Translated into English by Don Diego de Vades-forte 1640 Translated into French by René Moreau 1643 Translated into Latin by J.G. Volckamer 1644 Translated into English by J. Wadsworth 1652 Translated into Italian by A. Vitrioli 1667 Moreau's translation edited by Sylvestre Dufour 1671 and 1685 and translated into English by J. Chamberlaine 1685

[for titles, etc., see under translators]

DE VADES-FORTE, Don Diego. [The magnificent pseudonym of J. Wadsworth.] (Translated by.)

A CURIOUS TREATISE OF THE NATURE AND QUALITY OF CHOCOLATE by Antonio de Ledesma Colmenero. London 1640

MOREAU, René. (Translated by.)

DU CHOCOLAT DISCOURS CURIEUX by Antonio de Ledesma Colmenero. pp. 59. Paris 1643

[VOLCKAMER, J.G. Translated by.]

CHOCOLATA INDA, OPUSCULUM DE QUALITATE ET NATURA CHOCOLATAE by Antonio de Ledesma Colmenero. pp. 73. Norimbergae 1644

(In same volume with this is "Opobalsamum Orientalae" and "Pisonis Observationes Medicae." Total pp. 224.)

WADSWORTH, J. (Translated by.)

CHOCOLATE: OR AN INDIAN DRINKE ETC. by Antonio Ledesma Colmenero. London 1652

STUBBE(S), Henry.

THE INDIAN NECTAR OR A DISCOURSE CONCERNING CHOCOLATA. pp. 184. London 1662

BRANCATIUS, Franciscus Maria.

DE CHOCALATIS POTU DIATRIBE. pp. 36. Rome 1664

PAULLI, Simon.

COMMENTARIUS DE ABUSU TABACI THEE. Argentorati (see 1746) 1665

VITRIOLI, A. (Translated by.)

DELLA CIOCCOLATA DISCORSO. [From Moreau's translation of Colmenero's book.] Rome 1667

SEBASTUS MELISSENUS, F. Nicephorus.

DE CHOCOLATIS POTIONE RESOLUTIO MORALIS. pp. 36. Naples 1671

SYLVESTRE DUFOUR, P. [Edited by.]

DE L'USAGE DU CAPHÉ, DU THÉ, ET DU CHOCOLAT. pp. 188. Lyon 1671

[The part on chocolate, pp. 59, is a revision of Moreau's translation of Colmenero's book, plus B. Marradon's dialogue on chocolate.]

Translated into English by J. Chamberlaine (which see). 1685

HUGHES, William.

THE AMERICAN PHYSITIAN ... WHEREUNTO IS ADDED A DISCOURSE ON THE CACAO-NUT-TREE, AND THE USE OF ITS FRUIT, WITH ALL THE WAYS OF MAKING CHOCOLATE. London 1672

AUTHOR NOT GIVEN.

DESCRIPTION AND MANAGEMENT OF THE COCOA TREE. Phil. Trans. Abr. II. pp. 59. 1673

BONTEKOE, Willem.

Sundry short treatises in Dutch on Cocoa and Chocolate. about 1679

AUTHOR NOT GIVEN.

THE NATURAL HISTORY OF COFFEE, TEA, CHOCOLATE, TOBACCO AND ALSO THE WAY OF MAKING MUM. pp. 39. Printed for Christopher Wilkinson. London 1682

[Condemns chocolate on account of its containing "such a corrosive salt" as sugar. Mum is a peculiar kind of beer made from wheat malt.]

MUNDY, Henry.

OPERA OMNIA MEDICO-PHYSICA DE AËRE VITALI, ESCULENTIS ET POTULENTIS CUM APPENDICE DE PARERGIS IN VICTU ET CHOCOLATU, THEA, CAFFEA, TOBACCO. Oxford 1680. Leyden 1685

SYLVESTRE DUFOUR, P.

TRAITEZ NOUVEAUX ET CURIEUX DU CAFÉ, DU THÉ ET DU CHOCOLAT.

[The treatise on chocolate is compiled from the Spanish of Colmenero and B. Marradon.] pp. 403. à la Haye 1685 (With additions by St. Disdier) pp. 404. à la Haye 1693 Published by Deville. pp. 404. Lyon 1688

The above in Latin (by J. Spon), "TRACTATUS NOVI DE POTU CAPHE, DE CHIENSIUM, THE, ET DE CHOCOLATA." pp. 202. Paris 1685

A further Latin translation of the above, "NOVI TRACTATUS DE POTU CAPHE, DE CHIENSIUM, THE, ET DE CHOCOLATA." pp. 188. Geneva 1699

CHAMBERLAINE, J. (Translated by.)

THE MANNER OF MAKING COFFEE, TEA AND CHOCOLATE.
pp. 116. London 1685

[A translation of Sylvestre Dufour's compilation, the part on
Chocolate entitled "A Curious Treatise of the Nature and Quality
of Chocolate," being a translation of Colmenero's book.]

BLEGNY, Nicholas de.

LE BON USAGE DE THÉ, DU CAFFÉ, ET DU CHOCOLAT
POUR LA PRESERVATION ET POUR LA GUERISON DES
MALADES. pp. 358. Paris 1687 pp. 358. Lyon 1687

MAPPUS, Marcus.

DISSERTATIONES MEDICAE TRES DE RECEPTIS HODIE
ETIAM IN EUROPA, POTUS CALIDI GENERIBUS THÉE,
CAFÉ, CHOCOLATA. pp. 66. Argentorati 1695

1701-1800

DUNCAN, Dr.

WHOLESOME ADVICE AGAINST THE ABUSE OF HOT
LIQUORS, PARTICULARLY OF COFFEE, TEA, CHOCOLATE,
ETC. pp. 280. London 1706

AUTHOR NOT GIVEN [by De Chélus.]

HISTOIRE NATURELLE DU CACAO ET DU SUCRE. pp. 227.
Paris 1719 pp. 228. Amsterdam 1720 pp. 404. Amsterdam 1720
pp. 95. London 1724

BROOKES, R. [the above by De Chélus.] (Translated by.)

NATURAL HISTORY OF CHOCOLATE. pp. 95. Printed for J. Roberts, London 1724 pp. 95. Printed for Browne, London 1725 pp. 95. Printed for J. Roberts, London 1730

ACT OF PARLIAMENT, George II, 1723.

Relating to "LAYING INLAND DUTIES ON COFFEE, TEA AND CHOCOLATE." London 1724

BRUCKMAN, F.E.

RELATIO DE CACAO. Brunswick 1738

BARON, H.T.

AN SENIBUS CHOCOLATAE PUTUS? Paris 1739

PAULI, S. [PAULLI.]

A TREATISE ON TOBACCO, TEA, COFFEE AND CHOCOLATE. Translated by Dr. James. pp. 171. London (see 1665) 1746

N.N. [pseudonym of D. CONGINA.]

MEMORIE STORICHE SOPRA L'USO DELLA CIOCCOLATA IN TEMPO DI DIGIUNO ETC. Historical memoir on the use of chocolate upon fast days. pp. 196. Venice 1748

STAYLEY, G.

THE CHOCOLATE MAKERS OR MIMICKRY EXPOSED. An Interlude. Dublin. 1759

AUTHOR NOT GIVEN.

OBSERVATIONS SUR LE CACAO ET SUR LE CHOCOLAT.
pp. 144. Paris 1772

SMITH, Hugh.

AN ESSAY ON FOREIGN TEAS, WITH OBSERVATIONS ON
MINERAL WATERS, COFFEE, CHOCOLATE, ETC. London
1794

1801-1900

PARMENTIER

ON THE COMPOSITION AND USE OF CHOCOLATE.
Nicholson's Journal. London 1803

GALLAIS, A.

MONOGRAPHIE DU CACAO. pp. 216. Paris 1827

MITSCHERLICH, A.

DER KAKAO UND DIE SCHOKOLADE. Berlin 1859

GOSSELIN, A.

MANUEL DES CHOCOLATIERS. pp. 53. Paris 1860

MANGIN, A.

LE CACAO ET LA CHOCOLAT. Paris 1862

HEWETT, C. (of Messrs. Dunn and Hewett.)

CHOCOLATE AND COCOA, GROWTH AND PREPARATION.
pp. 88. London 1862

COMPAGNIE COLONIALE.

CHOCOLATE: ITS CHARACTER AND HISTORY. pp. 37. Paris 1868

HOLM, J.

COCOA AND ITS MANUFACTURE. Rivers, London.

SINCLAIR, W.J.

BEVERAGES, TEA, COCOA, ETC. (Health Lectures, Vol. 4). Manchester 1881

SALDAU, E.

DIE CHOCOLADE-FABRIKATION. pp. 232. Vienna (see 1907) 1881

MORRIS, D.

CACAO: HOW TO GROW IT. pp. 45. Jamaica (see 1887) 1882

TRINIDAD Agricultural Association.

CURING OF COCOA DISCUSSED. pp. 6. 1885

BARTELINK, E.J.

HANDLEIDING VOOR KAKAO-PLANTERS. pp. 68. Amsterdam 1885

English Translation, "THE CACAO PLANTERS' MANUAL." pp. 57. London 1885

BAKER, W., & Co.

COCOA AND CHOCOLATE. pp. 152. Dorchester, Mass., U.S.A. (see 1891 and 1899) 1886

MORRIS, D.

CACAO: HOW TO GROW IT. pp. 42. Jamaica (see 1882) 1886

ZIPPERER, P.

DIE CHOCOLADE FABRIKATION. pp. 181. Berlin (see 1902 and 1913) 1889

BANNISTER, R.

CANTOR LECTURES ON SUGAR, COFFEE, TEA AND COCOA. pp. 77. London 1890

BAKER, W., & Co.

THE CHOCOLATE PLANT AND ITS PRODUCTS. pp. 40. Dorchester, Mass., U.S.A. (see 1886 and 1899) 1891

HART, J.H.

CACAO. pp. 77. Port of Spain, Trinidad (see 1900 and 1911) 1892

HATTON, J.

COCOA. pp. 22. London 1892

HISTORICUS.

COCOA: ALL ABOUT IT. pp. 114. London (see 1896) 1892

GORDIAN, A.

DIE DEUTSCHE SCHOKOLADEN UND ZUCKERWAREN INDUSTRIE. Hartleben's Verlag. Hamburg 1895

ROQUE, L. De Belfort de la.

GUIDE PRATIQUE DE LA FABRICATION DU CHOCOLAT. Paris 1895

HISTORICUS.

COCOA: ALL ABOUT IT. pp. 99. London (see 1892) 1896

VILLON.

MANUEL DU CONFISEUR ET DU CHOCOLAT. Paris 1896

GOLDOS, L.

MANNUAL DE FABRICACIÓN INDUSTRIAL DE CHOCOLATE. pp. 261. Madrid 1897

OLIVIERI, F.E.

CACAO PLANTING AND ITS CULTIVATION. pp. 34. Port of Spain, Trinidad (see 1903) 1897

EPPS, James.

THE CACAO PLANT. pp. 11. (Transactions Croydon Microscopical and Natural History Club) 1898

BAKER, W., & Co.

COCOA AND CHOCOLATE. pp. 71. Dorchester, Mass., U.S.A. (see 1886 and 1891) 1899

HART, J.H.

CACAO. pp. 117. Port of Spain, Trinidad (see 1892 and 1911) 1900

JUMELLE, H.

LE CACOYER: SA CULTURE ET SON EXPLOITATION. pp. 211. Paris 1900

MENIER.

HISTORIQUE DES ÉTABLISSEMENTS MENIER. (Printed for Exposition Universelle.) pp. 44. Paris 1900

MODERN WORKS, 1901-1920.

(a) Cacao Cultivation.

SMITH, H. Hamel.

SOME NOTES ON COCOA PLANTING IN THE WEST INDIES. pp. 70 1901

WILDEMAN, E. de.

LES PLANTES TROPICALES DE GRANDE CULTURE--CAFE, CACAO, ETC. pp. 304. Bruxelles 1902

PREUSS, Paul.

EXPEDITION NACH CENTRAL UND SÜD-AMERIKA. Berlin.

French translation of part of the above, "LE CACAO, CULTURE ET PREPARATION" (from Bulletin Société d'Etudes Coloniales). pp. 249. 1902

EITLING, C.

DER KAKAO, SEINE KULTUR UND BEREITUNG. pp. 39. 1903

OLIVIERI, F.E.

TREATISE ON CACAO. pp. 101. Trinidad (see 1897) 1903

KINDT, L.

DIE KULTUR DES KAKAOBAUMES UND SEINE SCHÄDLINGE. pp. 157. Hamburg 1904

STEUART, M.E.

EVERYDAY LIFE ON A CEYLON COCOA ESTATE. pp. 256. London 1905

CHALOT, C. and LUC, M.

LE CACOYER AU CONGO FRANCAIS. pp. 58 1906

FAUCHERE, A.

CULTURE PRATIQUE DU CACAOYER ET PREPARATION DU CACAO. pp. 175. Paris 1906

PRUD'HOMME, E.

LE COCOTIER. CULTURE, INDUSTRIE ET COMMERCE. pp. 491. 1906

DE MENDONCA, Monteiro.

BOA ENTRADA PLANTATIONS, SAN THOMÉ. pp. 63. London 1907

MOUNTMORRES, Viscount.

MAIZE, COCOA, RUBBER. pp. 44. Liverpool 1907

SALDAU, E.

DIE SCHOKOLADEN FABRIKATION. Vienna (see 1881) 1907

WRIGHT, H.

THEOBROMA CACAO OR COCOA. pp. 249. Colombo 1907

RAFAELI, V., and MAXIMILIANO, E.

HOW JOSÉ FORMED HIS CACAO ESTATE. pp. 18. Trinidad 1907

TORAILLE, C.F.

STOLEN FROM THE FIELDS. A TREATISE ON CACAO AND ITS CULTIVATION. Trinidad 1907

HUGGINS, J.D.

HINTS TO THOSE ENGAGING IN THE CULTIVATION OF COCOA. pp. 24. Port of Spain, Trinidad 1908

SMITH, H. Hamel.

THE FUTURE OF CACAO PLANTING. pp. 95. London 1908

ATBE.

EL CULTIVO LAS DISERSAS INDUSTRIAS DES COCO. pp. 42. Quito 1909

HART, J.H.

CACAO. pp. 307. Duckworth, London (see 1892 and 1900) 1911

SMITH, H. Hamel.

NOTES ON SOIL AND PLANT SANITATION ON CACAO AND RUBBER ESTATES. pp. 603. Bale, London 1911

CARVATHO, d'Almeida.

A ILHA DE S. THOME E A AGRICULTURA PROGRESSIVA. (Includes Culturas de Cacoeiro.) pp. 228. Lisbon 1912

JOHNSON, W.H.

COCOA: ITS CULTIVATION AND PREPARATION. pp. 186. (Imperial Institute.) London 1912

AUTHOR NOT GIVEN.

CACAO CULTURE IN THE WEST INDIES. pp. 75. Havana. (Published by German Alkali Works, Cuba.) 1912

HENRY, Yves.

LE CACAO. pp. 103. Paris 1913

SMITH, H. Hamel.

THE FERMENTATION OF CACAO. pp. 318. Bale, London 1913

MALINS-SMITH, W.M.

PRACTICAL CACAO PLANTING IN GRENADA. (*West India Committee Circular*, April to December.) 1913

HALL, C.J.J. van.

COCOA. pp. 512. Macmillan, London 1914

KNAPP, A.W.

THE PRACTICE OF CACAO FERMENTATION. pp. 24. Bale, London 1914

(*b*) *Chocolate Manufacture.*

BESSELICH, N.

DIE SCHOKOLADE. pp. 74. Trier.

ZIPPERER, P.

MANUFACTURE OF CHOCOLATE. pp. 277. Berlin, London and New York (see 1889 and 1913) 1902

DUVAL, E.

CONFISERIE MODERNE. 1908

BOOTH, N.P., CRIBB, C.H., and ELLIS-RICHARDS, P.A.

THE COMPOSITION AND ANALYSIS OF CHOCOLATE. Reprinted from the *Analyst.* pp. 15. London 1909

FRITSCH, F.

FABRICATION DU CHOCOLAT. pp. 349. Paris 1910

FRANCOIS, L.

LES ALIMENTS SUCRES INDUSTRIELS (Chocolats, Bonbons, etc.) pp. 143. Paris 1912

WHYMPER, R.

COCOA AND CHOCOLATE: THEIR CHEMISTRY AND MANUFACTURE. pp. 327. Churchill, London 1912

ZIPPERER, P.

DIE SCHOKOLADEN-FABRIKATION. pp. 349. Berlin (see also 1889 and 1902) 1913

JACOUTOT, Auguste.

CHOCOLATE AND CONFECTIONERY MANUFACTURE. pp. xv, 211. J. Baker & Sons. London

(c) General.

WINTON, A.L., SILVERMAN, M., and BAILEY, E.M.

[ANALYSES OF CACAO AND COCOA.] Report Connecticut Agri. Expt. Station, U.S.A. pp. 40. 1902

HEAD, Brandon.

THE FOOD OF THE GODS. pp. 109. London 1903

STOLLWERCK, W.

DER KAKAO UND DIE SCHOKOLADEN INDUSTRIE. pp. 102. Jena 1907

U.S. CONSULAR REPORT NO. 50 (Dept. of Commerce and Labour.)

COCOA PRODUCTION AND TRADE. pp. 51. Washington 1912

CASTILLO, Ledon.

EL CHOCOLATE. pp. vi, 30. Mexico 1917

BULLETIN IMPERIAL INSTITUTE.

COCOA PRODUCTION IN THE BRITISH EMPIRE. pp. 40-95. London 1919

KNAPP, A.W., and McLELLAN, B.G.

THE ESTIMATION OF CACAO SHELL (reprint from *Analyst*). pp. 21. London 1919

* * * * *

The bibliography above is made as complete as possible as far as bound books in English are concerned. It also gives the more important continental publications. Should any errors or omissions have been made here or elsewhere, the author will be grateful if readers will point them out.

PERIODICALS.

Only one or two of the important papers in current literature are mentioned. Much valuable material is to be found in the following:

CACAO PRODUCTION

The papers published by the various departments of agriculture (especially those of Trinidad, Grenada, Philippines, Java, Ceylon, Gold Coast, Kew, etc.), the *Bulletin of the Imperial Institute*, *The West India Committee Circular*, *Tropical Life*, *West*

Africa, Der Tropenpflanzer, etc.

STATISTICS

The Gordian, Tea and Coffee Trade Journal.

MANUFACTURE

The Confectioners' Union.

CHEMISTRY

The Analyst, the *Journal of the Society of Chemical Industry*, and the *Journal of the Chemical Society.*

INDEX

Asterisks denote illustrations.

THE WESTMINSTER PRESS HARROW ROAD LONDON

Updated editions will replace the previous one--the old editions will be renamed.

Creating the works from public domain print editions means that no one owns a United States copyright in these works, so the Foundation (and you!) can copy and distribute it in the United States without permission and without paying copyright royalties. Special rules, set forth in the General Terms of Use part of this license, apply to copying and distributing Project Gutenberg-tm electronic works to protect the PROJECT GUTENBERG-tm concept and trademark. Project Gutenberg is a registered trademark, and may not be used if you charge for the eBooks, unless you receive specific permission. If you do not charge anything for copies of this eBook, complying with the rules is very easy. You may use this eBook for nearly any purpose such as creation of derivative works, reports, performances and research. They may be modified and printed and given away--you may do practically ANYTHING with public domain eBooks. Redistribution is subject to the trademark license, especially commercial redistribution.

*** START: FULL LICENSE ***

THE FULL PROJECT GUTENBERG LICENSE PLEASE READ THIS BEFORE YOU DISTRIBUTE OR USE THIS WORK

To protect the Project Gutenberg-tm mission of promoting the free distribution of electronic works, by using or distributing this work (or any other work associated in any way with the phrase "Project Gutenberg"), you agree to comply with all the terms of the Full Project Gutenberg-tm License (available with this file or online at http://gutenberg.org/license).

Section 1. General Terms of Use and Redistributing Project Gutenberg-tm electronic works

1.A. By reading or using any part of this Project Gutenberg-tm electronic work, you indicate that you have read, understand, agree to and accept all the terms of this license and intellectual property (trademark/copyright) agreement. If you do not agree to abide by all the terms of this agreement, you must cease using and return or destroy all copies of Project Gutenberg-tm electronic works in your possession. If you paid a fee for obtaining a copy of or access to a Project Gutenberg-tm electronic work and you do not agree to be bound by the terms of this agreement, you may obtain a refund from the person or entity to whom you paid the fee as set forth in paragraph 1.E.8.

1.B. "Project Gutenberg" is a registered trademark. It may only be used on or associated in any way with an electronic work by people who agree to be bound by the terms of this agreement. There are a few things that you can do with most Project Gutenberg-tm electronic works even without complying with the full terms of this agreement. See paragraph 1.C below. There are a lot of things you can do with Project Gutenberg-tm electronic works if you follow the terms of this agreement and help preserve free future access to Project Gutenberg-tm electronic works. See paragraph 1.E below.

1.C. The Project Gutenberg Literary Archive Foundation ("the Foundation" or PGLAF), owns a compilation copyright in the collection of Project Gutenberg-tm electronic works. Nearly all the individual works in the collection are in the public domain in the United States. If an individual work is in the public domain in the United States and you are located in the United States, we do not claim a right to prevent you from copying, distributing, performing, displaying or creating derivative works based on the work as long as all references to Project Gutenberg are removed. Of course, we hope that you will support the Project Gutenberg-tm mission of promoting free access to electronic works by freely sharing Project Gutenberg-tm works in compliance with the terms of this agreement for keeping the

Project Gutenberg-tm name associated with the work. You can easily comply with the terms of this agreement by keeping this work in the same format with its attached full Project Gutenberg-tm License when you share it without charge with others.

1.D. The copyright laws of the place where you are located also govern what you can do with this work. Copyright laws in most countries are in a constant state of change. If you are outside the United States, check the laws of your country in addition to the terms of this agreement before downloading, copying, displaying, performing, distributing or creating derivative works based on this work or any other Project Gutenberg-tm work. The Foundation makes no representations concerning the copyright status of any work in any country outside the United States.

1.E. Unless you have removed all references to Project Gutenberg:

1.E.1. The following sentence, with active links to, or other immediate access to, the full Project Gutenberg-tm License must appear prominently whenever any copy of a Project Gutenberg-tm work (any work on which the phrase "Project Gutenberg" appears, or with which the phrase "Project Gutenberg" is associated) is accessed, displayed, performed, viewed, copied or distributed:

This eBook is for the use of anyone anywhere at no cost and with almost no restrictions whatsoever. You may copy it, give it away or re-use it under the terms of the Project Gutenberg License included with this eBook or online at www.gutenberg.org

1.E.2. If an individual Project Gutenberg-tm electronic work is derived from the public domain (does not contain a notice indicating that it is posted with permission of the copyright holder), the work can be copied and distributed to anyone in the

United States without paying any fees or charges. If you are redistributing or providing access to a work with the phrase "Project Gutenberg" associated with or appearing on the work, you must comply either with the requirements of paragraphs 1.E.1 through 1.E.7 or obtain permission for the use of the work and the Project Gutenberg-tm trademark as set forth in paragraphs 1.E.8 or 1.E.9.

1.E.3. If an individual Project Gutenberg-tm electronic work is posted with the permission of the copyright holder, your use and distribution must comply with both paragraphs 1.E.1 through 1.E.7 and any additional terms imposed by the copyright holder. Additional terms will be linked to the Project Gutenberg-tm License for all works posted with the permission of the copyright holder found at the beginning of this work.

1.E.4. Do not unlink or detach or remove the full Project Gutenberg-tm License terms from this work, or any files containing a part of this work or any other work associated with Project Gutenberg-tm.

1.E.5. Do not copy, display, perform, distribute or redistribute this electronic work, or any part of this electronic work, without prominently displaying the sentence set forth in paragraph 1.E.1 with active links or immediate access to the full terms of the Project Gutenberg-tm License.

1.E.6. You may convert to and distribute this work in any binary, compressed, marked up, nonproprietary or proprietary form, including any word processing or hypertext form. However, if you provide access to or distribute copies of a Project Gutenberg-tm work in a format other than "Plain Vanilla ASCII" or other format used in the official version posted on the official Project Gutenberg-tm web site (www.gutenberg.org), you must, at no additional cost, fee or expense to the user, provide a copy, a means of exporting a copy, or a means of obtaining a copy upon request, of the work in its original "Plain Vanilla ASCII" or other form. Any alternate format must include the full Project Gutenberg-tm License as specified in paragraph 1.E.1.

1.E.7. Do not charge a fee for access to, viewing, displaying, performing, copying or distributing any Project Gutenberg-tm works unless you comply with paragraph 1.E.8 or 1.E.9.

1.E.8. You may charge a reasonable fee for copies of or providing access to or distributing Project Gutenberg-tm electronic works provided that

- You pay a royalty fee of 20% of the gross profits you derive from the use of Project Gutenberg-tm works calculated using the method you already use to calculate your applicable taxes. The fee is owed to the owner of the Project Gutenberg-tm trademark, but he has agreed to donate royalties under this paragraph to the Project Gutenberg Literary Archive Foundation. Royalty payments must be paid within 60 days following each date on which you prepare (or are legally required to prepare) your periodic tax returns. Royalty payments should be clearly marked as such and sent to the Project Gutenberg Literary Archive Foundation at the address specified in Section 4, "Information about donations to the Project Gutenberg Literary Archive Foundation."

- You provide a full refund of any money paid by a user who notifies you in writing (or by e-mail) within 30 days of receipt that s/he does not agree to the terms of the full Project Gutenberg-tm License. You must require such a user to return or destroy all copies of the works possessed in a physical medium and discontinue all use of and all access to other copies of Project Gutenberg-tm works.

- You provide, in accordance with paragraph 1.F.3, a full refund of any money paid for a work or a replacement copy, if a defect in the electronic work is discovered and reported to you within 90 days of receipt of the work.

- You comply with all other terms of this agreement for free distribution of Project Gutenberg-tm works.

1.E.9. If you wish to charge a fee or distribute a Project Gutenberg-tm electronic work or group of works on different terms than are set forth in this agreement, you must obtain permission in writing from both the Project Gutenberg Literary Archive Foundation and Michael Hart, the owner of the Project Gutenberg-tm trademark. Contact the Foundation as set forth in Section 3 below.

1.F.

1.F.1. Project Gutenberg volunteers and employees expend considerable effort to identify, do copyright research on, transcribe and proofread public domain works in creating the Project Gutenberg-tm collection. Despite these efforts, Project Gutenberg-tm electronic works, and the medium on which they may be stored, may contain "Defects," such as, but not limited to, incomplete, inaccurate or corrupt data, transcription errors, a copyright or other intellectual property infringement, a defective or damaged disk or other medium, a computer virus, or computer codes that damage or cannot be read by your equipment.

1.F.2. LIMITED WARRANTY, DISCLAIMER OF DAMAGES - Except for the "Right of Replacement or Refund" described in paragraph 1.F.3, the Project Gutenberg Literary Archive Foundation, the owner of the Project Gutenberg-tm trademark, and any other party distributing a Project Gutenberg-tm electronic work under this agreement, disclaim all liability to you for damages, costs and expenses, including legal fees. YOU AGREE THAT YOU HAVE NO REMEDIES FOR NEGLIGENCE, STRICT LIABILITY, BREACH OF WARRANTY OR BREACH OF

CONTRACT EXCEPT THOSE PROVIDED IN PARAGRAPH F3.
YOU AGREE THAT THE FOUNDATION, THE TRADEMARK
OWNER, AND ANY DISTRIBUTOR UNDER THIS
AGREEMENT WILL NOT BE LIABLE TO YOU FOR ACTUAL,
DIRECT, INDIRECT, CONSEQUENTIAL, PUNITIVE OR
INCIDENTAL DAMAGES EVEN IF YOU GIVE NOTICE OF THE
POSSIBILITY OF SUCH DAMAGE.

1.F.3. LIMITED RIGHT OF REPLACEMENT OR REFUND - If
you discover a defect in this electronic work within 90 days of
receiving it, you can receive a refund of the money (if any) you
paid for it by sending a written explanation to the person you
received the work from. If you received the work on a physical
medium, you must return the medium with your written
explanation. The person or entity that provided you with the
defective work may elect to provide a replacement copy in lieu of
a refund. If you received the work electronically, the person or
entity providing it to you may choose to give you a second
opportunity to receive the work electronically in lieu of a refund. If
the second copy is also defective, you may demand a refund in
writing without further opportunities to fix the problem.

1.F.4. Except for the limited right of replacement or refund set
forth in paragraph 1.F.3, this work is provided to you 'AS-IS'
WITH NO OTHER WARRANTIES OF ANY KIND, EXPRESS OR
IMPLIED, INCLUDING BUT NOT LIMITED TO WARRANTIES
OF MERCHANTIBILITY OR FITNESS FOR ANY PURPOSE.

1.F.5. Some states do not allow disclaimers of certain implied
warranties or the exclusion or limitation of certain types of
damages. If any disclaimer or limitation set forth in this
agreement violates the law of the state applicable to this
agreement, the agreement shall be interpreted to make the
maximum disclaimer or limitation permitted by the applicable
state law. The invalidity or unenforceability of any provision of
this agreement shall not void the remaining provisions.

1.F.6. **INDEMNITY**

- You agree to indemnify and hold the Foundation, the trademark owner, any agent or employee of the Foundation, anyone providing copies of Project Gutenberg-tm electronic works in accordance with this agreement, and any volunteers associated with the production, promotion and distribution of Project Gutenberg-tm electronic works, harmless from all liability, costs and expenses, including legal fees, that arise directly or indirectly from any of the following which you do or cause to occur: (a) distribution of this or any Project Gutenberg-tm work, (b) alteration, modification, or additions or deletions to any Project Gutenberg-tm work, and (c) any Defect you cause.

Section 2. Information about the Mission of Project Gutenberg-tm

Project Gutenberg-tm is synonymous with the free distribution of electronic works in formats readable by the widest variety of computers including obsolete, old, middle-aged and new computers. It exists because of the efforts of hundreds of volunteers and donations from people in all walks of life.

Volunteers and financial support to provide volunteers with the assistance they need, is critical to reaching Project Gutenberg-tm's goals and ensuring that the Project Gutenberg-tm collection will remain freely available for generations to come. In 2001, the Project Gutenberg Literary Archive Foundation was created to provide a secure and permanent future for Project Gutenberg-tm and future generations. To learn more about the Project Gutenberg Literary Archive Foundation and how your efforts and donations can help, see Sections 3 and 4 and the Foundation web page at http://www.pglaf.org.

Section 3. Information about the Project Gutenberg Literary Archive Foundation

The Project Gutenberg Literary Archive Foundation is a non profit 501(c)(3) educational corporation organized under the laws of the state of Mississippi and granted tax exempt status by the Internal Revenue Service. The Foundation's EIN or federal tax identification number is 64-6221541. Its 501(c)(3) letter is posted at http://pglaf.org/fundraising. Contributions to the Project Gutenberg Literary Archive Foundation are tax deductible to the full extent permitted by U.S. federal laws and your state's laws.

The Foundation's principal office is located at 4557 Melan Dr. S. Fairbanks, AK, 99712., but its volunteers and employees are scattered throughout numerous locations. Its business office is located at 809 North 1500 West, Salt Lake City, UT 84116, (801) 596-1887, email business@pglaf.org. Email contact links and up to date contact information can be found at the Foundation's web site and official page at http://pglaf.org

For additional contact information: Dr. Gregory B. Newby Chief Executive and Director gbnewby@pglaf.org

Section 4. Information about Donations to the Project Gutenberg Literary Archive Foundation

Project Gutenberg-tm depends upon and cannot survive without wide spread public support and donations to carry out its mission of increasing the number of public domain and licensed works that can be freely distributed in machine readable form accessible by the widest array of equipment including outdated equipment. Many small donations ($1 to $5,000) are particularly important to maintaining tax exempt status with the IRS.

The Foundation is committed to complying with the laws regulating charities and charitable donations in all 50 states of the United States. Compliance requirements are not uniform and it takes a considerable effort, much paperwork and many fees to meet and keep up with these requirements. We do not solicit donations in locations where we have not received written confirmation of compliance. To SEND DONATIONS or determine the status of compliance for any particular state visit http://pglaf.org

While we cannot and do not solicit contributions from states where we have not met the solicitation requirements, we know of no prohibition against accepting unsolicited donations from donors in such states who approach us with offers to donate.

International donations are gratefully accepted, but we cannot make any statements concerning tax treatment of donations received from outside the United States. U.S. laws alone swamp our small staff.

Please check the Project Gutenberg Web pages for current donation methods and addresses. Donations are accepted in a number of other ways including checks, online payments and credit card donations. To donate, please visit: http://pglaf.org/donate

Section 5. General Information About Project Gutenberg-tm electronic works.

Professor Michael S. Hart is the originator of the Project Gutenberg-tm concept of a library of electronic works that could be freely shared with anyone. For thirty years, he produced and distributed Project Gutenberg-tm eBooks with only a loose network of volunteer support.

Project Gutenberg-tm eBooks are often created from several printed editions, all of which are confirmed as Public Domain in the U.S. unless a copyright notice is included. Thus, we do not necessarily keep eBooks in compliance with any particular paper edition.

Most people start at our Web site which has the main PG search facility:

http://www.gutenberg.org

This Web site includes information about Project Gutenberg-tm, including how to make donations to the Project Gutenberg Literary Archive Foundation, how to help produce our new eBooks, and how to subscribe to our email newsletter to hear about new eBooks.

Cocoa and Chocolate, by Arthur W. Knapp

A free ebook from http://manybooks.net/

www.ingramcontent.com/pod-product-compliance
Lightning Source LLC
Chambersburg PA
CBHW062003280526
45787CB00005B/1980